The Power of Being Alone for Men

Discovering Inner Strength and Success Through Solitude

© **Copyright 2024 - All rights reserved.**

The content contained within this book may not be reproduced, duplicated, or transmitted without direct written permission from the author or the publisher.

Under no circumstances will any blame or legal responsibility be held against the publisher or author for any damages, reparation, or monetary loss due to the information contained within this book, either directly or indirectly.

Legal Notice:

This book is copyright-protected. It is only for personal use. You cannot amend, distribute, sell, use, quote, or paraphrase any part of the content within this book without the consent of the author or publisher.

Disclaimer Notice:

Please note the information contained within this document is for educational and entertainment purposes only. All effort has been executed to present accurate, up-to-date, reliable, and complete information. No warranties of any kind are declared or implied. Readers acknowledge that the author is not engaging in the rendering of legal, financial, medical, or professional advice. The content within this book has been derived from various sources. Please consult a licensed professional before attempting any techniques outlined in this book.

By reading this document, the reader agrees that under no circumstances is the author responsible for any losses, direct or indirect, that are incurred as a result of the use of the information contained within this document, including, but not limited to, errors, omissions, or inaccuracies.

Table of Contents

Introduction 1

Chapter 1: Introduction to the Topic 3

Chapter 2: Understanding Solitude 16

Chapter 3: The Psychology of Solitude 35

Chapter 4: Navigating Relationships 56

Chapter 5: Harnessing Creativity and
Productivity 80

Chapter 6: Cultivating Inner Strength 105

Chapter 7: Embracing Solitude in
Modern Life 129

Chapter 8: The Journey Ahead 160

Conclusion 183

References 186

Introduction

Society tells men to be strong, stoic, and constantly connected. However, what if that constant pressure to be "on" leaves you feeling drained, unfulfilled, and even a little lost?

The truth is, there's a hidden power in being alone. It's a power that unlocks a more fulfilling life, stronger relationships, and a deeper sense of purpose.

The Power of Being Alone for Men will help you reclaim your time, understand the science behind solitude, and harness it as a tool for transformation.

Why This Book Is Different:

- **Uncomplicated and Actionable:** Forget dense psychology jargon and vague practices. This book is written in a clear, concise style that's easy to understand, even for beginners. You'll be equipped with practical, hands-on methods to integrate solitude into your daily life.

- **Tailored for Men:** Many self-help books offer generic advice that doesn't resonate with men's unique challenges. This book explores the specific social pressures and emotional complexities that men grapple with, providing targeted strategies for overcoming them through the power of solitude.

- **Unlock Your Potential:** Do you feel creatively stifled or emotionally drained? This book will help you harness the power of solitude to fuel your creativity, boost your productivity, and cultivate inner strength. You'll tap into a wellspring of inspiration and build resilience simply by embracing some "me time."

- **Build Stronger Relationships:** Contrary to popular belief, solitude isn't the enemy of connection. It's the foundation for building healthier, more meaningful relationships. This guide will show you how to cultivate a strong relationship with yourself, the first step towards attracting and nurturing genuine connections with others.

- **Scientifically Backed:** This book explores the science behind why solitude is crucial for mental well-being and emotional resilience. You'll discover how embracing "alone time" improves focus, reduces stress, and boosts overall happiness.

The Power of Being Alone for Men isn't just another self-help book. It's a transformative journey towards a life filled with purpose, strength, and authentic connection. Are you ready to unlock the power within you?

Chapter 1: Introduction to the Topic

Have you ever felt a pang of guilt for wanting some "me time?" In today's hyper-connected world, the pressure to be constantly available is immense. However, what if there's a hidden power in solitude, a secret weapon waiting to be unleashed? This chapter introduces the concept of solitude, exploring its true meaning and dispelling the negative connotations often associated with it, particularly for men. You'll uncover the surprising stigma surrounding male solitude and why embracing "alone time" is incredibly beneficial.

1. *Spend alone time. Source: https://www.pexels.com/photo/thoughtful-young-black-guy-resting-in-outdoor-cafe-6140703/*

Defining Solitude and Its Importance

In today's hyper-connected world, the very idea of solitude feels alien. You constantly navigate a social landscape of instant messaging, overflowing inboxes, and the pressure to be available 24/7. Yet, amidst this constant buzz, solitude is a powerful tool for personal growth and well-being. Often misunderstood and even feared, solitude is not about withdrawing from life or becoming a hermit. It's about embracing the power of being alone, of carving out dedicated time to disconnect from external noise and reconnect with yourself.

Solitude vs. Loneliness

Many people confuse solitude with loneliness. Loneliness is a distressing feeling of isolation and a lack of connection with others. It is a state of unwanted solitude. In contrast, solitude is a conscious choice to be alone, a state of being comfortable in your own company. It's a time for introspection, reflection, and rejuvenation. While loneliness drains your energy, solitude replenishes it.

The Power of Introspection

Solitude provides a fertile ground for introspection. Away from the constant external stimuli, you can finally hear your inner voice. This self-reflection allows you to process emotions, understand your motivations, and gain clarity on your goals. It's a space for honest self-evaluation, where you identify your strengths and weaknesses without the pressure of external expectations.

A Historical Perspective

Across cultures and throughout history, major philosophical and spiritual traditions have embraced solitude. From the solitary meditations of ancient Greek philosophers to the monastic practices of various religions, solitude has been recognized as a catalyst for personal growth and spiritual development. Whether it's the quiet contemplation of a Zen Garden or the solitary retreat of a writer seeking inspiration, solitude has been a cornerstone of human progress and self-discovery.

Masculinity Beyond Constant Connection

Societal expectations often portray men as needing constant social interaction to be strong and fulfilled. This pressure to be "always on" is stifling. Solitude allows you to break free from these outdated stereotypes. By embracing "alone time," you'll explore your emotional landscape without judgment, fostering deeper self-awareness and emotional intelligence.

Carving Out Space in a Chaotic World

This fast-paced, technology-driven world makes carving out time for solitude a challenge. The constant barrage of notifications and the pressure to be available leave little room for quiet introspection. However, this makes the pursuit of solitude even more important. By setting boundaries and prioritizing time for yourself, you create a sacred space to recharge, reconnect with your inner world, and ultimately, become a more present and engaged individual in all aspects of your life.

Exploring the Stigma Surrounding Male Solitude

In a world that celebrates constant connection and busyness, the idea of a man seeking solitude is often met with raised eyebrows and unspoken judgments. This stigma surrounding male solitude is a deeply ingrained societal construct that hinders men's well-being and reinforces outdated notions of masculinity.

Debunking the Myth

The most pervasive myth is the belief that a man seeking solitude is weak or unmanly. This stereotype paints a one-dimensional picture of masculinity, equating social connection with strength and vulnerability with weakness. It implies that men need the constant validation and energy of others to feel fulfilled. However, the reality is far more nuanced.

History is brimming with examples of strong and successful men who embraced solitude. From the stoic meditations of Roman Emperors like Marcus Aurelius to the introspective genius of artists like Vincent van Gogh, solitude has catalyzed self-discovery and achievement.

2. *Roman Emperors like Marcus Aurelius prioritized solitude that has self-discovery. Source: Glyptothek, Public domain, via Wikimedia Commons. https://commons.wikimedia.org/wiki/File:Marcus_Aurelius_Glyptothek_M%C3%BCnchen.jpg*

Throughout history, thinkers, inventors, and leaders have utilized solitude to hone their craft, process complex ideas, and strategize effectively. Imagine a world without the quiet contemplation of a scientist like Isaac Newton or the introspective genius of a writer like J. D. Salinger. Their solitude wasn't a sign of weakness but a necessary element in their creative process.

The truth is that strength lies not in the constant outward projection of masculinity but in the courage to be vulnerable with oneself. Solitude allows you to explore your emotions, fears, and desires without judgment. It allows you to recharge and reconnect with your inner strength, ultimately making you a more emotionally mature and resilient individual.

Examining the Emotional Burden

Society often casts men in the role of the emotional rock, expected to be strong and stoic and the sole provider of emotional support for others. This pressure to be a constant source of strength is incredibly burdensome. Solitude offers a much-needed respite from this emotional burden.

Just as physical strength requires periods of rest and recovery, so too does emotional resilience. In solitude, you process your emotions, deal with stress, and come to terms with your vulnerabilities without needing to present a facade of unwavering strength.

This introspective space allows you to better understand your emotional landscape, fostering self-compassion and emotional intelligence. This, in turn, strengthens your ability to connect with others on a deeper level and offer genuine emotional support when needed.

Fear of Missing Out (FOMO)

The modern world's constant connectivity fuels a pervasive fear of missing out (FOMO). With a curated glimpse into the seemingly perfect lives of others on social media, you feel anxious while choosing to be alone. You might worry that others are having more fun, achieving more success, or forming deeper connections while you're opting for solitude.

This pressure to be constantly engaged is a recipe for anxiety and dissatisfaction. Understand that carefully crafted online personas don't represent reality. Solitude allows you to detach from this constant comparison trap and reconnect with your priorities and values. It provides a space to reflect on what truly matters to you, allowing you to pursue your goals and aspirations without being swayed by external validation.

Moreover, the FOMO associated with solitude often stems from misunderstanding its purpose. Solitude isn't about withdrawing from life entirely; it's about creating space for intentional connection. By prioritizing time for yourself, you return to your relationships feeling refreshed and energized, fostering more meaningful and fulfilling connections.

Social Media and the "Comparison Trap"

Social media plays a significant role in perpetuating the stigma surrounding male solitude. The carefully curated feeds filled with images of exciting events, vibrant social lives, and seemingly effortless successes create a distorted picture of reality.

Men who choose solitude might feel left behind, inadequate, or even ostracized for not conforming to the constant "on-the-go" lifestyle portrayed online. Social media is a highlight reel, not a reflection of everyday life.

Solitude prevents you from this distorted portrayal of happiness and success. It provides a space to define your metrics for fulfillment, focusing on personal growth, self-discovery, and genuine connection rather than chasing an illusion projected through filters and carefully crafted captions.

Breaking Free from Societal Expectations

The root of the stigma surrounding male solitude lies in outdated notions of masculinity. Traditional expectations dictate that you should be strong, emotionless, and constantly available to others. It's time to break free from these restrictive definitions and embrace a more nuanced understanding of masculinity.

True strength lies not in denying your emotions or the constant need for social validation but in the courage to be vulnerable, the ability to connect with yourself, and the pursuit of personal growth. Solitude empowers you to redefine masculinity on your terms.

Ultimately, embracing solitude is not about rejecting social connection. It's about creating a healthy balance. By prioritizing time for yourself, you'll return to your relationships, careers, and social lives feeling refreshed, more engaged, and renewed sense of purpose.

The Potential Benefits of Embracing Solitude for Men

Carving out time for solitude in a world that bombards you with constant stimuli feels counterintuitive. Yet, solitude offers a treasure trove of benefits for men seeking personal growth and a richer life experience. Stepping away from the constant noise and busyness allows you to reconnect with yourself, unleash your creativity, and cultivate a deeper sense of well-being.

Enhanced Mental Clarity

On a cluttered desk overflowing with papers and unfinished tasks, it's difficult to concentrate on any single item in that chaotic environment. Similarly, your mind, bombarded with notifications, emails, and social media updates, often lacks the necessary space for focused thinking. Solitude provides a much-needed decluttering for the mind.

Free from distractions, you enter a state of deep concentration, where thoughts become clearer, and the ability to focus sharpens. This enhanced mental clarity allows you to tackle complex tasks more efficiently, analyze information with greater detail, and make sound decisions. Solitude improves working memory and cognitive flexibility, leading to better problem-solving skills and increased productivity.

Just as an athlete needs dedicated quiet time to practice their skills and refine their movements, solitude provides a space for you to train your mind, hone your focus, and become a more effective thinker.

Deeper Self-Awareness

The constant hum of social interaction drowns the whispers of your inner voice. Solitude provides a precious opportunity to silence external noise and reconnect with your authentic self. In the quiet space of "alone time", you discover yourself.

Free from the pressure to conform to social expectations, you explore your values, desires, and motivations without external influence. This introspective space allows a deeper understanding of who you are at your core, what truly matters to you, and what you want to achieve.

3. Reflecting through journaling cultivates deeper self-awareness. Source: https://www.pexels.com/photo/elderly-man-writing-on-a-journal-5710595/

By reflecting on your experiences and emotions in solitude, you'll identify your strengths and weaknesses, develop a greater sense of self-compassion, and ultimately, make choices that align with your authentic selves. This journey of self-awareness empowers you to live a life true to your values and aspirations.

Boosted Creativity

Solitude has long been a muse for artists, writers, and inventors. The quiet contemplation away from distractions is a breeding ground for groundbreaking ideas. History is filled with examples of creative geniuses who harnessed the power of solitude to unlock their potential. The solitary walks of Beethoven in nature, the quiet meditations of Steve Jobs, and the introspective retreats of J. K. Rowling are just a few testaments to the power of solitude in igniting creativity.

Free from the pressure to conform or the fear of judgment, men in solitude can explore new ideas without reservation. You can tap into your subconscious mind, discover unconventional thoughts, and experiment with different creative approaches. This introspective space allows for a free flow of ideas, sparking innovation and fueling creative pursuits.

Whether composing a symphony, writing a novel, or designing a new invention, solitude provides a fertile ground where creativity blossoms. By embracing solitude, you'll unleash your inner artist and unlock your full creative potential.

Strengthened Emotional Intelligence

In a world that often encourages you to suppress or ignore your emotions, solitude offers a safe space to process them effectively. Away from the judgment of others, you explore your emotional landscape without fear. You'll acknowledge difficult emotions like anger, sadness, or fear, understand their root causes, and develop healthy coping mechanisms.

This introspective journey fosters emotional intelligence, a crucial skill for navigating the complexities of human relationships. By understanding your emotions, you'll better understand the emotions of others. This allows you to develop empathy, build stronger connections with loved ones, and communicate with greater emotional maturity.

Solitude isn't about becoming emotionless stoics. It's about acknowledging and processing emotions healthily. Through this process, you develop the emotional intelligence to connect with others on a deeper level, fostering more meaningful and fulfilling relationships.

Greater Confidence and Resilience

The fear of being alone is a significant hurdle for men new to embracing solitude. However, overcoming this fear and learning to be comfortable in your own company is a key step toward building self-reliance and inner strength.

Solitude challenges you to confront your anxieties about isolation and loneliness. By actively spending time alone and enjoying it, you cultivate a sense of self-sufficiency and independence. This newfound confidence spills over into all aspects of life, empowering you to navigate challenges more resiliently and pursue your goals with unwavering determination.

Just as physical strength increases with consistent exercise, emotional resilience strengthens with the practice of solitude. By confronting your fear of being alone and learning to enjoy your own company, you build an inner strength that allows you to bounce back from setbacks and weather life's uncertainties with greater confidence.

This newfound resilience is crucial for navigating the complexities of professional and personal life. It allows you to stand up for yourself, assert your needs, and navigate conflict with greater composure.

A Catalyst for Transformation

The benefits of embracing solitude for men are far-reaching. It fosters enhanced mental clarity, allowing you to think more effectively and solve problems creatively. It provides a space for self-discovery, leading to a deeper understanding of your values and aspirations. It sparks innovation, fueling creative pursuits and igniting groundbreaking ideas. It strengthens emotional intelligence, enabling you to build stronger, more meaningful relationships. Finally, it builds self-reliance and inner strength, empowering you to navigate life's challenges with greater confidence and resilience.

Solitude is not a luxury but a necessity. By carving out dedicated time for yourself, you unlock your full potential and experience a richer, more fulfilling life. It's a journey of self-discovery, a wellspring of creativity, and a foundation for emotional well-being.

This Journey of Embracing Solitude Is Not Without Its Challenges: You might initially feel uncomfortable with the silence, unsure how to fill the "alone time" you've created. It's important to approach solitude with a sense of exploration and experimentation. Start small, carve out dedicated time for yourself, even for just 15 minutes a day. Use this time for introspection, reading, pursuing hobbies, or simply enjoying the quiet space.

Solitude Is a Journey, Not a Destination: There will be days when social interaction is fulfilling and others when solitude is deeply needed. By embracing both, you'll cultivate a richer, more fulfilling life that celebrates authentic connection, self-discovery, and the power of being alone.

By now, you may be intrigued by the idea of solitude but still a little hesitant. Rest assured; this book isn't advocating for social isolation. Instead, it will unlock the transformative power of solitude. In the coming chapters, you'll explore the science behind why being alone is crucial for mental well-being, discover how historical figures and modern-day leaders have harnessed its power, and find practical strategies to integrate solitude into your own life. So, get ready to break free from the constant noise and unlock the amazing potential that lies within.

Chapter 2: Understanding Solitude

You finally have a moment to yourself. No notifications pinging or emails demanding attention, just you and your own company. Sounds peaceful, right? However, for some men, the idea of solitude is daunting. Is it the same as feeling lonely? Is it a sign of weakness? This chapter dives into the heart of solitude, untangling its true meaning and exploring how it can be a powerful tool for personal growth. You'll also explore how different cultures view male independence and how some of history's greatest minds harnessed the power of being alone.

4. *Understand the difference between solitude and loneliness. Source: https://www.pexels.com/photo/unrecognizable-man-sitting-on-rooftop-edge-against-cloudy-sundown-sky-5780744/*

Differentiating Between Loneliness and Solitude

Loneliness and solitude are often used interchangeably, creating a significant misunderstanding. While both involve being alone, the emotional and social context creates a stark distinction. Understanding this difference is crucial before embracing solitude as a path to personal growth.

Characteristics of Loneliness: A Yearning for Connection

Loneliness is a pervasive feeling of isolation and disconnection from others. It's a yearning for meaningful relationships that remain unfulfilled. It's like having a void in your social circle, a constant ache for a sense of belonging. Negative emotions like sadness, emptiness, and anxiety often accompany loneliness. These feelings significantly impact your overall well-being, leaving you feeling unseen, unheard, and unsupported.

Loneliness Manifests in Various Ways

- **Social Anxiety:** The fear of social interaction prevents you from forming connections, leading to a vicious cycle of isolation and loneliness. Social events might feel overwhelming, and initiating conversations can be daunting.

- **Feeling Like an Outsider:** You might be surrounded by people but feel a constant disconnect as if you don't truly belong. This can happen in social groups, work environments, or romantic relationships.

- **Difficulty Maintaining Relationships:** You might struggle to initiate or maintain close connections. Conversations might feel forced, leading to emotional distance from others.

The Benefits of Connection: Humans Are Wired for Social Interaction

Humans are social creatures who thrive on connection. Healthy social relationships provide a foundation for emotional well-being and a sense of purpose. Here are some key benefits of strong social bonds:

- **A Sense of Belonging:** Feeling like you belong to a community provides a vital sense of security and reduces feelings of isolation. It allows you to be yourself, knowing you're accepted and supported for who you are.

- **Social Support:** Strong social bonds offer a network of support during difficult times. Knowing you have people to rely on for a listening ear, a shoulder to cry on, or a helping hand can significantly improve your ability to cope with life's challenges. Conversely, having loved ones to share your joy with during celebrations deepens the experience.

- **Different Perspectives:** Healthy relationships expose you to different viewpoints and experiences, enriching your understanding of the world. It allows you to challenge your own biases, learn from others, and grow as individuals. Hearing how others cope with similar situations or navigate challenges provides valuable insights and broadens your perspective.

Social interaction is a vital aspect of the human experience. While solitude can be a powerful tool, neglecting social connection can have detrimental effects.

Identifying Your Needs: Solitude vs. Loneliness

Feeling the need to be alone doesn't automatically mean you're lonely. Here's how to identify your true needs:

- **Do You Crave Meaningful Social Interaction?** If the answer is yes, and the thought of spending time alone fills you with dread, you might be struggling with loneliness and need to focus on building supportive connections. Consider joining clubs or groups aligned with your interests or reconnecting with old friends.

- **Do You Feel Drained and Overwhelmed by Social Interaction?** If so, you might need solitude to recharge and reconnect with yourself. Listen to your body's cues. Do you feel a surge of anxiety at the thought of social gatherings or find yourself needing to withdraw after extended periods of socializing?

- **Do You Feel a Sense of Peace and Rejuvenation When Alone?** This signifies that you're embracing healthy solitude, not succumbing to loneliness. Solitude allows you to process your thoughts and emotions freely, fostering a sense of clarity and inner peace. You might be more focused, creative, and productive after dedicated "alone time."

Building a Support System: Cultivating Healthy Relationships

Even while embracing solitude, strong social connections are essential. Here's how to build a healthy support system:

- **Invest in Existing Relationships:** Nurture your connection with close friends and family members. Make time for regular check-ins, share your thoughts and feelings openly, and be there for them as well. Let them know you value their presence in your life.

- **Expand Your Social Circle:** Explore new hobbies or join groups that align with your interests, creating opportunities to meet like-minded people. Don't hesitate to step outside your comfort zone and initiate conversations with new people. Strike up a conversation with someone at the gym, join an online forum related to your hobbies, or take a class to learn a new skill.

- **Focus on Quality over Quantity:** Prioritize a few deep and meaningful connections over a large circle of superficial acquaintances. True friendships offer genuine support, understanding, and a sense of belonging. Invest time and energy in fostering close bonds with people who share your values and make you feel accepted and appreciated.

*5. Quality over quantity. Source:
https://www.pexels.com/photo/group-of-people-sitting-on-white-mat-on-grass-field-745045/*

When to Seek Help: Recognizing Chronic Loneliness

While occasional feelings of loneliness are normal, chronic loneliness can have a significant impact on your physical and mental health. Here are some signs that professional support might be needed:

- **Persistent Loneliness:** If feelings of isolation and disconnection persist despite efforts to build social connections, it might be a sign of underlying issues like social anxiety or depression. Reaching out to a therapist can help you understand the root cause of your loneliness and develop strategies for overcoming it.

- **Negative Impact on Daily Life:** If loneliness significantly impacts your daily life, hindering your ability to work, socialize, or enjoy activities you once found pleasurable, professional support can be crucial.

- **Physical Health Problems:** Chronic loneliness can manifest physically, leading to sleep disturbances, changes in appetite, and a weakened immune system. If you're experiencing unexplained physical symptoms alongside persistent loneliness, consult a doctor or therapist to rule out any underlying medical conditions and develop a plan to address the emotional aspect.

- **Suicidal Thoughts:** If feelings of loneliness become overwhelming and lead to thoughts of self-harm or suicide, seeking immediate professional help is critical. There are resources available to help you through this difficult time. You are not alone.

Seeking professional support for loneliness is not a sign of weakness but a sign of strength and a willingness to invest in your well-being. A therapist will equip you with the tools and strategies to overcome loneliness and build meaningful connections.

Solitude and loneliness are distinct experiences. While solitude offers a path to self-discovery and rejuvenation, chronic loneliness harms one's well-being. By understanding the difference and acknowledging your needs, you'll embrace solitude as a tool for personal growth while nurturing your social connections to build a fulfilling life.

Cultural and Societal Perspectives on Male Independence

Throughout history, and even in contemporary society, the concept of male independence has been burdened by contradictory expectations. While solitude is a cornerstone of self-discovery and emotional well-being for men, it often clashes with ingrained cultural ideals. Here, you explore the complex tapestry of societal pressures and the evolving landscape of male independence.

The "Strong Silent Type": A Flawed Ideal

For generations, the cultural archetype of the "strong, silent type" has dominated societal expectations of masculinity. This image portrays men as stoic, unemotional figures who find strength in solitude but struggle to express vulnerability.

- **Emotional Suppression:** This ideal promotes the suppression of emotions, leading you to believe that seeking solace in solitude equates to weakness.

- **Disconnection from Others:** The pressure to be emotionally reserved hinders you from forming deep and meaningful connections, creating a sense of isolation despite being physically present in social settings.

- **Difficulty Processing Emotions:** If you bottle up emotions, you might struggle to process them healthily, leading to emotional outbursts or difficulty coping with stress and setbacks.

This outdated ideal fails to recognize the vast spectrum of healthy masculinity. True strength lies not in the denial of emotions but in the ability to navigate them with self-awareness and healthily express them.

The Pressures of Conformity: The Social Butterfly Myth

Societal pressure often dictates that you must be a social butterfly, thriving in large groups and constantly engaging in outward activity. This expectation can be stifling if you naturally crave solitude for introspection and rejuvenation.

- **Fear of Judgment:** Men who embrace solitude might face social disapproval or be perceived as withdrawn or anti-social. This fear of judgment prevents you from prioritizing time alone, hindering your self-discovery and emotional well-being.

- **The "Busy" Badge of Honor:** Society often equates busyness and constant social engagement with success. You might feel pressured to maintain a packed schedule, neglecting the importance of dedicated "alone time" for reflection and growth.

- **Missing Out (FOMO):** The constant barrage of social media showing seemingly perfect and exciting social lives fuels FOMO (fear of missing out). You might feel guilty for choosing solitude, believing you're missing out on valuable experiences or social connections.

It is crucial to recognize that the need for solitude doesn't equate to social ineptitude. You can be both independent and enjoy social interaction. The key lies in honoring your needs and striking a healthy balance between solitude and social engagement.

The Evolving Landscape: Embracing Vulnerability

Fortunately, the tide is turning. Today, there's a growing acceptance of male vulnerability and emotional expression.

- **Breaking the Mold:** Celebrities, athletes, and public figures are increasingly sharing their experiences with mental health challenges and the importance of self-care. This openness dismantles the myth of the invulnerable man and normalizes the need for solitude and emotional exploration.

- **Men's Support Groups:** The rise of men's support groups creates safe spaces for men to connect, share experiences, and challenge traditional notions of masculinity. These groups foster a sense of belonging and empower men to embrace their individuality and emotional needs.

- **Focus on Mental Health:** Mental health awareness campaigns highlight the importance of self-care and emotional well-being for everyone, regardless of gender. This shift in focus allows men to prioritize their mental health without fear of judgment or societal disapproval.

The growing acceptance of male vulnerability is creating a more nuanced understanding of masculinity, paving the way for a future where men can embrace solitude and self-discovery without societal constraints.

Finding Your Tribe: Surrounding Yourself with Supportive Peers

Men who value solitude also need supportive social connections with like-minded individuals.

- **Seek Out Men Who Embrace Vulnerability:** Surrounding yourself with comfortable men who express their emotions and prioritize self-care creates a safe space for open communication and shared experiences.

- **Explore Communities of Interest:** Joining hobby groups, online forums, or clubs related to your passions allows you to connect with men who share your interests and provide a platform for meaningful social interaction.

- **Challenge Stereotypes within Existing Friendships:** Open conversations with your existing friends about the importance of solitude and emotional expression can lead to a more supportive and understanding social circle.

Finding your tribe of supportive men fosters a sense of belonging and allows you to embrace your individuality without fear of judgment.

Leading by Example: Redefining Masculinity for Future Generations

You have the opportunity to redefine masculinity for future generations. By embracing solitude and emotional well-being, you can challenge outdated stereotypes.

- **Openly Discuss Your Needs:** Talking openly about your need for solitude and self-care will normalize these behaviors for younger generations.

- **Model Healthy Emotional Expression:** By healthily expressing your emotions, you demonstrate to young men that vulnerability is not a sign of weakness but a strength that fosters deeper connections.

- **Challenge Stereotypes in Media:** Call out media portrayals that perpetuate outdated notions of masculinity. Support content that celebrates diverse expressions of manhood, including the value of self-reflection and emotional intelligence.

By leading by example, you'll create a world where future generations embrace solitude and emotional well-being without societal constraints.

Cultural and societal perspectives on male independence have been complex and often contradictory. However, the landscape is evolving. The growing acceptance of male vulnerability and emotional expression is paving the way for a future where men can embrace solitude as a path to self-discovery and personal growth while fostering healthy social connections. By challenging outdated stereotypes and leading by example, you'll redefine masculinity for future generations, creating a world that celebrates the full spectrum of what it means to be a man.

Historical Figures and Their Relationship with Solitude

Solitude isn't a new concept. Throughout history, some of humanity's greatest minds, creatives, and leaders have sought out solitude, recognizing its power to fuel their work, refine their vision, and achieve greatness. Here, you'll discover the fascinating relationship between historical figures and solitude.

Philosophers and Thinkers

For philosophers and thinkers, solitude provides a fertile ground for intellectual exploration and the development of groundbreaking ideas.

- **Aristotle:** One of the greatest philosophers of ancient Greece, Aristotle believed that "solitude is sometimes necessary for the production of our best work." He advocated for dedicated periods of contemplation, away from distractions, as a crucial element for philosophical inquiry.

- **Marcus Aurelius:** The Roman emperor and Stoic philosopher is known for his "Meditations," a series of personal writings reflecting on themes of virtue, duty, and the human condition. These profound reflections were likely honed during his periods of solitude spent contemplating life's complexities.

6. *Aristotle believed that "solitude is sometimes necessary for the production of our best work." Source: See page for author, CC BY 4.0 <https://creativecommons.org/licenses/by/4.0>, via Wikimedia Commons. https://commons.wikimedia.org/wiki/File:Aristotle_refusing_the_hemlock_(%3F)._Oil_painting_by_a_painte_Wellcome_L0019669.jpg*

For a scholar surrounded by the bustle of a marketplace, the constant chatter, the clamor of vendors, the jostling crowds would be far from ideal for deep philosophical contemplation. Solitude, on the other hand, allows philosophers to explore their thoughts without distractions. They can analyze information from various perspectives, wrestle with complex ideas, and ultimately formulate their unique contributions to their field.

Artists and Creatives

Solitude has long been a muse for artists and creatives of all disciplines.

- **Ludwig van Beethoven:** The famed composer famously retreated to the countryside to compose some of his most renowned works. The quiet solitude allowed him to tap into his creativity and translate his emotions into music. Beethoven could fully immerse himself in the creative process without the pressures of social engagements and external expectations. The quiet introspection allowed him to explore unconventional melodies, experiment with different harmonies, and, ultimately, craft masterpieces that continue to resonate with audiences centuries later.

- **Vincent van Gogh:** This Dutch post-impressionist painter often worked in solitude, immersing himself in nature and drawing inspiration from his surroundings. The quiet contemplation fostered by solitude allowed van Gogh to connect with his inner world and express his emotions through vibrant colors and bold brushstrokes.

For artists, solitude isn't just about escaping distractions. It's about creating a space for exploration and vulnerability. Free from the judgment of critics or the pressure to conform to artistic trends, you discover your emotions, experiment with techniques, and tap into the depths of your creativity to produce truly unique and emotionally evocative works.

Leaders and Visionaries

Even in the bustling world of leadership, solitude is a valuable tool.

- **Mahatma Gandhi:** The champion of nonviolent resistance spent significant periods in solitude, practicing meditation and reflection. This introspection helped him refine his strategies and strengthen his resolve in the fight for Indian independence. Away from the constant demands of political life, Gandhi could discover his moral compass, contemplate the ethical implications of his actions, and emerge with a renewed sense of purpose and clarity.

- **Nelson Mandela:** During his 27 years of imprisonment, Nelson Mandela turned to solitude for solace and reflection. He used this time to educate himself, refine his vision for a free South Africa, and emerge as a powerful leader for social justice. In the quiet solitude of his prison cell, Mandela could analyze the political landscape, strategize for the future, and maintain his spirit of resilience in the face of immense adversity.

For leaders, solitude offers a space for strategic planning beyond their roles' immediate demands. It allows them to reflect on past actions, analyze the effectiveness of their strategies, and, ultimately, develop a clear vision for the future. This introspection helps them make sound decisions, navigate complex situations with wisdom, and inspire those around them.

Spiritual Leaders and Ascetics

Many religious traditions emphasize the importance of solitude for spiritual growth and enlightenment.

- **Monastic Life:** Monks, nuns, and ascetics throughout history have chosen to live a life of seclusion, dedicating themselves to prayer, meditation, and spiritual contemplation. Solitude allows them to connect with a higher power and better understand themselves and the universe. Removed from the temptations and distractions of the material world, they can focus their entire being on their spiritual journey.

- **Vision Quests:** In many indigenous cultures, individuals embark on solitary journeys into nature to seek guidance and spiritual insight. This withdrawal from society allows them to commune with nature, confront their inner demons, and receive messages from the spirit world. In the quiet solitude of the wilderness, they can strip away external influences and connect with their true selves, returning with a renewed sense of purpose and a deeper understanding of their place in the world.

The Power of Disconnection: Retreats and Purposeful Withdrawal

The concept of retreats and purposeful withdrawal from society isn't reserved for historical figures or spiritual leaders. Today, individuals from all walks of life recognize the value of disconnecting from technology and the constant busyness of modern life.

- **Meditation Retreats:** These retreats offer a structured environment for focused meditation practice, allowing participants to dive deep into their inner world and cultivate inner peace. Solitude allows you to quiet the mind, let go of distractions, and connect with your true self on a deeper level.

- **Digital Detoxes:** In today's hyper-connected world, taking a break from technology is crucial for mental well-being and fostering a connection with the present moment. Disconnecting from the constant stream of emails, social media updates, and notifications allows you to reconnect with yourself, your loved ones, and the natural world around you.

Purposeful withdrawal isn't about abandoning social responsibility or neglecting your duties. It's about creating dedicated spaces for introspection, self-discovery, and rejuvenation. By embracing temporary periods of solitude, you return to your daily life with renewed clarity, focus, and a deeper appreciation for the world around you.

Historical figures across various fields have recognized the immense power of solitude. From philosophers seeking wisdom to artists unleashing their creativity and leaders honing their strategies, solitude has played a crucial role in human achievement and personal growth. By understanding how these figures embraced solitude, you'll unlock its potential in your life, fostering a path to self-discovery, increased creativity, and a deeper understanding of yourself and the world around you.

By now, you should have a clearer picture of solitude and how it differs from the dreaded feeling of loneliness. You've seen how cultures have shaped your understanding of male independence and how historical figures embraced solitude to achieve greatness. In the next chapter, you'll dive deeper into the psychology of solitude, exploring the science behind why being alone is crucial for mental well-being and emotional resilience.

Chapter 3: The Psychology of Solitude

By now, you've explored the very essence of solitude, differentiating it from loneliness and uncovering its historical significance. However, understanding the "why" behind solitude's power is just as crucial as the "how." This chapter explores the fascinating psychology of solitude, revealing the science behind its benefits and equipping you with the knowledge to unlock its transformative potential.

7. *Cultivate psychological well-being through solitude. Source: https://www.pexels.com/photo/photo-of-smiling-with-his-arms-wide-spread-1762611/*

You will explore the positive impacts of solitude on your mental well-being, from fostering self-reflection and emotional intelligence to aiding in overcoming anxieties associated with being alone. By understanding the internal shifts that occur during solitude, you'll harness its power for personal growth, improved mental clarity, and a deeper understanding of yourself.

More than just spending time alone, this journey of embracing solitude is about cultivating a deeper connection with your inner world. Buckle up, gentleman, as you discover the science of solitude and unlock the secrets to a richer, more fulfilling life.

Mental Health Benefits of Spending Time Alone

The constant stimulation of the modern world leaves you feeling overwhelmed and drained. This is where solitude steps in, offering a refuge for mental well-being and a springboard for personal growth. Here are some specific ways that solitude benefits your mental health.

Reducing Stress and Anxiety: Finding Peace in Quiet Contemplation

The constant barrage of information, social interactions, and demands on your time leave you feeling stressed and anxious. Solitude provides a much-needed escape from this external noise.

- **Relaxation Response:** When alone, your body shifts into a relaxation response. Heart rate slows, blood pressure decreases, and muscle tension eases, promoting a sense of calm and well-being.

- **Emotional Processing:** Solitude allows you to process difficult emotions without judgment. You acknowledge and work through feelings of anger, sadness, or frustration without the pressure of social expectations. By giving yourself space to feel these emotions, you prevent them from building up and negatively impacting your mental health.

- **Improved Sleep:** Chronic stress and anxiety significantly disrupt sleep patterns. Solitude allows you to unwind, clear your mind of worries, and prepare for a restful night's sleep. This, in turn, improves your overall mood, energy levels, and cognitive function.

- **Enhanced Resilience:** Confronting and processing difficult emotions in solitude develops greater emotional resilience. You learn to cope with challenges more effectively and bounce back from setbacks with greater strength.

Imagine being constantly bombarded by news updates, emails, and social media notifications. It's no wonder stress and anxiety take hold. Solitude provides a sanctuary, a space free from external pressures, allowing your body and mind to unwind and relax.

Improving Focus and Concentration: Quieting the Mind for Enhanced Clarity

Maintaining focus is challenging in this fast-paced world. Solitude offers a powerful tool for enhancing concentration and mental clarity.

- **Quieting the Mental Chatter:** When alone, you silence the constant internal dialogue and external distractions that fragment your attention. This allows you to focus your thoughts on a single task, improving your ability to learn new information, solve problems effectively, and complete projects more efficiently.

- **Deeper Thinking:** Free from distractions, you dive deeper into complex ideas and explore different perspectives. This fosters critical thinking skills and allows you to approach challenges with more creativity and insight.

- **Enhanced Creativity:** Solitude allows your mind to wander freely, fostering a state of mind conducive to creative breakthroughs. Without the pressure of immediate action or external expectations, you explore new ideas, make unexpected connections, and generate innovative solutions.

- **Improved Decision-Making:** Giving yourself space to reflect and process information without distractions helps you make clearer, more well-considered decisions. Solitude allows you to weigh the pros and cons of a situation objectively, reducing the influence of external pressures and biases.

Just like an athlete needs quiet time to prepare for a competition, your mind benefits from dedicated periods of solitude to focus and perform at its peak. By removing distractions, you'll truly concentrate on the task at hand, leading to improved productivity and a sense of accomplishment.

Boosting Self-Esteem: Overcoming the Fear of Being Alone

The fear of being alone is a significant barrier to embracing solitude. However, overcoming this fear and learning to enjoy your own company is a key step towards building self-confidence.

- **Self-Reliance:** Solitude allows you to develop a sense of self-reliance. You learn to rely on your thoughts and interests for entertainment and fulfillment, fostering a sense of independence and inner strength.

- **Appreciating Your Own Company:** By spending quality time alone, you appreciate your company and discover the unique qualities and interests that make you who you are. This self-acceptance and self-appreciation contribute to a healthy sense of self-esteem.

- **Inner Strength:** Confronting and overcoming the fear of being alone builds inner strength and emotional resilience. You learn that you are capable and resourceful, even without the constant presence of others.

- **Self-Discovery:** Solitude provides a space for self-discovery. Free from external influences, you can explore your thoughts, feelings, and values without judgment. This introspection leads to a deeper understanding of who you are and what you want in life.

- **Fulfillment:** This newfound sense of independence allows you to connect with others on a deeper level, fostering more meaningful relationships.

Learning to be comfortable in your own company is a powerful act of self-love that strengthens your sense of self-worth. It demonstrates that you are a complete and interesting person, capable of finding joy and fulfillment independent of external validation. This newfound confidence spills over into your interactions with others, allowing you to connect with greater authenticity and build stronger, more meaningful relationships.

Enhancing Creativity: Sparking Innovation in the Quiet

Solitude isn't just about relaxation; it's a catalyst for creativity.

- **Daydreaming and Boredom:** Solitude can lead to a state of daydreaming or boredom. This might seem unproductive, but it is crucial for creative thinking. Free from external stimulation, your mind wanders, making unexpected connections and generating new ideas.

- **Problem-Solving from Different Angles:** In solitude, you approach problems from different perspectives without the pressure of conforming to groupthink. This introspection allows you to identify novel solutions and generate innovative ideas that might not have emerged in a group setting.

- **Breaking Through Mental Blocks:** When stuck on a creative project, solitude provides the space to step away, clear your head, and return with fresh eyes. The quiet introspection helps you break through mental blocks and approach the challenge with renewed inspiration.

Imagine yourself in a brainstorming session. While valuable, such environments also stifle creativity due to the pressure to conform. Solitude allows you to explore unconventional ideas without judgment, fostering a space where innovation truly flourishes.

Developing Emotional Intelligence: Understanding Yourself Through Introspection

Rather than escaping emotions, solitude is about understanding them.

- **Identifying Your Emotions:** In the quiet solitude, you tune into your emotions and identify their root causes. This self-awareness allows you to develop a healthy relationship with your feelings and constructively express them.

- **Empathy Through Self-Understanding:** By understanding your own emotions, you develop greater empathy for the emotions of others. This self-awareness allows you to connect more deeply with others and build stronger relationships.

- **Emotional Regulation:** Solitude provides a space to practice emotional regulation. You learn to identify triggers for negative emotions, develop coping mechanisms, and respond to challenges calmly and assertively.
- **Healthy Boundaries:** Spending time alone allows you to reflect on your needs and values. This self-awareness empowers you to set healthy boundaries in your relationships, ensuring your well-being is protected.

Solitude is all about developing emotional intelligence. By understanding your emotions in solitude, you navigate your internal world more clearly and connect with others on a deeper, more meaningful level.

Developing Self-Reflection and Emotional Intelligence

Solitude is a powerful tool for fostering self-reflection and emotional intelligence. Embracing quiet introspection gives you a deeper understanding of your thoughts, feelings, and motivations. This self-awareness empowers you to navigate the complexities of life with greater clarity and build meaningful connections with others. Here are some ways to cultivate self-reflection and emotional intelligence during your solitude:

The Power of Journaling: Putting Pen to Paper for Self-Discovery

Journaling is a powerful tool for self-reflection. When you put pen to paper, you create a safe space to explore your thoughts and emotions without judgment.

- **Processing Emotions:** Journaling allows you to explore your emotions, identify their triggers, and explore healthy ways of expressing them. Writing down your feelings is cathartic, releasing pent-up emotions and promoting emotional well-being.

- **Identifying Patterns:** Regular journaling allows you to recognize patterns in your thoughts and behaviors. You might notice recurring themes or triggers for negative emotions. This self-awareness empowers you to make positive changes in your life.

- **Setting Goals and Tracking Progress:** Use your journal to set personal goals and track your progress. Solitude allows for focused reflection on your aspirations, and journaling helps you plan to achieve them. Reviewing your entries provides a sense of accomplishment and motivates you to stay on track.

- **Boosting Creativity:** Journaling is a springboard for creativity. Freewriting exercises, where you write continuously without stopping or editing, unlock new ideas and perspectives.

Journaling is a simple yet powerful tool for self-discovery. By dedicating dedicated time in solitude to writing down your thoughts and emotions, you gain valuable insights into your inner world and chart a course for personal growth.

Mindfulness and Meditation Practices: Cultivating Present-Moment Awareness and Inner Peace

Mindfulness and meditation practices significantly enhance your self-reflection and emotional intelligence.

- **Present-Moment Awareness:** Mindfulness techniques help you focus on the present moment without judgment. This allows you to observe your thoughts and emotions without getting caught up in them. By becoming more aware of your internal state, you respond to situations more thoughtfully and effectively.

- **Reduced Stress and Anxiety:** Regular meditation reduces stress and anxiety, allowing you to approach your emotions more clearly and calmly. In solitude, you fully immerse yourself in mindfulness exercises, promoting feelings of inner peace and emotional regulation.

- **Increased Self-Compassion:** Mindfulness practices cultivate self-compassion. By observing your thoughts and emotions without judgment, you learn to accept yourself with all your flaws and imperfections. This self-acceptance is crucial for developing healthy emotional intelligence.

Mindfulness and meditation are valuable tools for cultivating inner peace and emotional awareness. By incorporating these practices into your solitude routine, you can gain greater control over your emotional responses and navigate life's challenges more resiliently.

Connecting with Your Inner Child: Understanding Your Core Needs and Desires

Solitude provides a space to reconnect with your inner child, the part of you that holds onto your core needs and desires.

- **Identifying Unmet Needs:** During times of quiet reflection, you might discover unmet needs from your childhood that still impact your present-day behavior. Solitude allows you to explore these needs in a safe space and develop strategies for healthily fulfilling them.

- **Unlocking Creativity:** Your inner child is often brimming with creativity and enthusiasm. By reconnecting with this playful side, you tap into a wellspring of inspiration and joy, enriching your life in unexpected ways.

- **Developing Self-Compassion:** Understanding your inner child's vulnerabilities fosters self-compassion. By acknowledging your past experiences and unmet needs, you practice self-forgiveness and move forward with greater emotional clarity.

Solitude is a catalyst for self-improvement and self-acceptance. Connecting with your inner child brings a deeper understanding of your core needs and desires, fostering a sense of wholeness and emotional intelligence.

Embracing Vulnerability: Building Deeper Connections Through Open Communication

While solitude allows for introspection, emotional intelligence also requires the ability to connect with others. This necessitates embracing vulnerability and expressing your emotions openly.

- **Strengthening Relationships:** Sharing your feelings with trusted friends fosters deeper connections. Vulnerability allows others to see the authentic you and creates a space for genuine empathy and support.

- **Building Trust:** Open communication and emotional expression are essential for building trust in relationships. Allowing yourself to be vulnerable encourages others to do the same, fostering stronger and more meaningful connections.

- **Conflict Resolution:** By healthily expressing emotions, you navigate conflict with greater understanding and empathy. Vulnerability allows you to address issues directly, work towards solutions collaboratively, and strengthen your relationships.

- **Personal Growth:** Sharing your struggles and experiences with others is a powerful tool for personal growth. The feedback and support you receive offer valuable insights and help you navigate challenges with greater resilience.

Embracing vulnerability makes you aware of your weaknesses and strengths. By allowing yourself to be seen and heard authentically, you create a foundation for deeper connections and pave the way for personal growth.

Practicing Gratitude: Cultivating Positivity and Well-Being

Solitude can also be a space to cultivate gratitude, an essential component of emotional intelligence.

- **Shifting Perspective:** Taking time alone allows you to reflect on the positive aspects of your life, from your relationships to your accomplishments. This practice of gratitude shifts your perspective, fostering a sense of contentment and well-being.

- **Increased Happiness:** Gratitude has been scientifically linked to increased happiness and life satisfaction. Focusing on the good things in your life during solitude cultivates a more positive outlook and emotional resilience.

- **Strengthening Relationships:** Expressing gratitude to others strengthens your bonds with them. Taking time alone to reflect on the positive qualities of the people in your life allows you to express your appreciation more authentically, deepening your connections.

- **Appreciating the Simple Things:** Solitude allows you to slow down and appreciate the simple pleasures in life. By taking time to reflect in quiet contemplation, you develop a deeper appreciation for the beauty and wonder of the world around you.

Practicing gratitude is a powerful tool for cultivating emotional well-being and fostering positive relationships. By incorporating gratitude into your solitude routine, you develop a more optimistic outlook and handle life's challenges with greater resilience.

8. Appreciate the simple things. Source: https://www.pexels.com/photo/man-with-backpack-sitting-on-rock-in-mountains-19956439/

Overcoming Fear and Anxiety Associated with Solitude

For many men, the concept of solitude is daunting. The fear of being alone, the worry of boredom, or the anxiety of facing your inner thoughts are significant barriers to embracing solitude. However, by understanding the root of these anxieties and implementing practical strategies, you overcome these fears and unlock the transformative power of spending time alone.

Identifying Your Fears: Understanding the Root of the Discomfort

The first step to overcoming any fear is understanding its source. Here are some common anxieties associated with solitude:

- **Fear of Boredom:** Your fear of boredom might stem from a reliance on external stimulation. Perhaps you haven't discovered the joy of introspection or explored activities you enjoy alone. You might be surprised at how much fulfillment you find in simply being present with your thoughts and engaging in activities that spark your intrinsic curiosity.

- **Fear of Judgment:** The worry of being judged for spending time alone might be rooted in societal pressures to be constantly social. Solitude is seen as a weakness, leading to feelings of isolation and inadequacy. Challenge this narrative. Solitude is a sign of self-reliance and strength. It demonstrates your comfort with your own company and the ability to find fulfillment independent of external validation.

- **Fear of Difficult Emotions:** Solitude forces you to confront unresolved emotions. The fear of facing these emotions leads you to avoid spending time alone altogether. However, solitude provides a safe space to process difficult emotions without judgment. Acknowledging them in a quiet space, you develop healthy coping mechanisms and move forward with greater emotional clarity.

- **Fear of Missing Out (FOMO):** The constant barrage of social media showing others' exciting lives creates a fear of missing out when spending time alone. Social media only portrays a reel of curated highlights. Solitude allows you to focus on your experiences and create your enjoyment, whether reading a captivating book, taking a rejuvenating walk in nature, or pursuing a creative hobby you've been meaning to try.

By identifying the specific fears holding you back, you develop strategies for addressing them.

Challenging Negative Thoughts: Reframing Your Inner Critic

Once you've identified your anxieties, challenge the negative self-talk associated with solitude. Here are some common examples and how to reframe your thoughts:

- **Negative Thought:** "Being alone is boring." Reframe: "Solitude is an opportunity to explore my interests and discover new hobbies. Maybe I can finally try that pottery class I've been interested in."
- **Negative Thought:** "People will think I'm lonely if I spend time alone." Reframe: "Spending time alone is a sign of self-reliance and strength. It shows I'm comfortable with my own company."
- **Negative Thought:** "If I'm alone, I'll be overwhelmed by negative emotions." Reframe: "Solitude allows me to process my emotions

healthily. By acknowledging them in a quiet space, I can develop coping mechanisms and move forward."

- **Negative Thought:** "Everyone else is out having fun while I'm alone." Reframe: "FOMO is a myth. Social media only portrays a curated highlight reel. I can create my enjoyment during solitude, whether it's reading a thought-provoking book or taking a rejuvenating walk-in nature."

Challenge these negative thought patterns and replace them with empowering affirmations. By reframing your perspective, solitude becomes an opportunity for growth and self-discovery.

Embracing Discomfort: Stepping Outside Your Comfort Zone

Growth often occurs outside your comfort zone. While spending time alone might feel uncomfortable at first, with practice, it becomes a source of joy and self-discovery.

- Start Small: Begin with short periods of solitude and gradually increase the duration as you become more comfortable. For example, you could start with 15 minutes of quiet reading each morning and gradually extend it to an hour-long walk in nature over the weekend. Don't overwhelm yourself. Small, consistent steps are key to building a sustainable solitude practice.

- Focus on Activities You Enjoy: Engage in activities you find genuinely enjoyable during solitude. This could be anything that sparks your curiosity or brings you a sense of peace, whether reading a thought-provoking book, listening to a captivating podcast, working on a creative project you've been putting off, or simply journaling your thoughts and feelings. By associating solitude with fulfilling activities, you'll be more likely to look forward to your solo time.

Embrace the Quiet: Don't feel pressured to fill every moment with activity. Allow yourself to be present in the quiet and observe your thoughts and feelings without judgment. This quiet contemplation is a powerful tool for self-discovery. Sometimes, the greatest breakthroughs occur when you allow yourself to slow down and simply be.

Creating Safe Spaces: Cultivating a Sanctuary for Solitude

Your environment significantly impacts your experience of solitude. Here are some tips for creating a relaxing and enjoyable space for your solo time:

- **Find a Quiet Corner:** Dedicate a specific space in your home for solitude. It could be a cozy reading nook, a quiet corner on your balcony, or even a designated spot in a nearby park. This designated space will become a physical cue for your mind to shift into relaxation mode.

- **Minimize Distractions:** Turn off your phone notifications, silence your email alerts, and remove any devices that might tempt you to break your solitude. This dedicated time is for you to disconnect and reconnect with yourself.

- **Light Some Candles:** Create a calming ambiance with soft lighting or scented candles. Aromatherapy enhances relaxation and focus, making your solitude experience even more enjoyable.

- **Put on Some Relaxing Music:** Soft instrumental music or nature sounds create a peaceful atmosphere conducive to introspection and reflection. Choose music that complements your mood and allows you to unwind.

By creating a designated space for solitude and incorporating elements that promote relaxation, you transform your alone time into a truly enriching experience.

9. *Choose music that complements your mood and allows you to unwind. Source: https://www.pexels.com/photo/photo-of-man-using-headphones-3752835/*

Starting Small and Building Gradually: Embracing Solitude at Your Own Pace

Remember, embracing solitude is a journey, not a destination. Don't feel pressured to immediately jump into long periods of alone time.

- **Start with Short Sessions:** Begin with manageable chunks of solitude, gradually increasing the duration as you become more comfortable. Consistency is key. Even short periods of dedicated alone time yield significant benefits.

- **Listen to Your Body and Mind:** Pay attention to how you feel during and after your solitude sessions. If you feel overwhelmed or anxious, shorten the duration or adjust your activities. The goal is to create a positive association with solitude, so prioritize experiences that leave you feeling refreshed and rejuvenated.

- **Celebrate Your Progress:** Acknowledge your accomplishments, no matter how small. Reward yourself for incorporating solitude into your life, whether treating yourself to a relaxing bath after your reading session or enjoying a delicious cup of tea after your quiet walk-in nature.

By starting small, listening to your needs, and celebrating your progress, you cultivate a sustainable solitude practice that enriches your life and empowers you to navigate the world with greater clarity and emotional intelligence.

Throughout this chapter, you've explored the psychological underpinnings of solitude, shedding light on its profound impact on your mental well-being. From enhancing self-reflection and emotional intelligence to reducing anxiety and fostering creativity, the benefits of embracing solitude are undeniable.

Solitude is never about isolating yourself. It's about creating a space for intentional reflection and growth. Understanding the science behind solitude and its positive effects on your mind will equip you to integrate this powerful tool into your life.

Chapter 4: Navigating Relationships

The power of solitude extends far beyond personal well-being. It also has a profound impact on the quality of your relationships. This chapter explores the seemingly paradoxical concept of using solitude to strengthen your connections with others.

You will explore how effectively communicating your need for alone time fosters understanding and respect within your relationships. Furthermore, building independence through embracing solitude makes you a more well-rounded and engaging partner, friend, or family member. Finally, you'll tackle the art of balancing social interactions with solitary activities, ensuring you reap the benefits of both worlds.

10. Communicate your need for alone time. Source: https://www.pexels.com/photo/a-man-and-woman-talking-together-4347481/

Prepare to unpack the counterintuitive yet powerful truth that solitude isn't about withdrawing from life. It's about cultivating the emotional intelligence and self-awareness necessary to build stronger, more meaningful relationships.

Communicating the Need for Alone Time

One of the biggest hurdles men face when embracing solitude is the fear of being misunderstood or appearing disconnected from loved ones. However, open and honest communication is key to navigating this challenge. Here are some strategies to effectively communicate your need for alone time and foster understanding within your relationships:

Open and Honest Communication: Expressing Your Needs with Clarity

The first step is to clearly and respectfully express your need for solitude. Here are some tips:

- **Choose the Right Time:** Pick a calm and relaxed moment when you can have a focused conversation. Avoid bringing it up during arguments or stressful situations.

- **Focus on "I" Statements:** Instead of accusatory statements like "You need to give me some space," explain your need from your perspective. For example, "After a long day, I need some quiet time to recharge and feel my best."

- **Explain the Benefits:** Let your loved ones understand how solitude benefits you and strengthens your relationship. Briefly explain how spending time alone helps you manage stress, be more present together, and cultivate a sense of well-being that spills over into your interactions with others.

- **Offer Examples:** Provide specific examples of how your alone time translates into positive outcomes for the relationship. Mention how time alone helps you clear your head and approach problems with a calmer, more solution-oriented mindset. You could also explain how solitude allows you to recharge your creativity, leading to more engaging date nights or fun activities planned for the family.

- **Be Receptive to Feedback:** Listen attentively to your loved one's perspective. Maybe they have concerns about your need for solitude. Be open to discussing these concerns and finding solutions that work for both of you.

Open and honest communication fosters understanding and reduces the risk of feeling misunderstood. You create a space for open dialogue and collaboration by clearly expressing your needs.

Setting Healthy Boundaries: Establishing Limits Without Guilt

Communicating your need for solitude also involves setting healthy boundaries. Here's how:

- **Be Specific:** Instead of a vague request for "alone time," specify what that looks like for you. Do you need an hour after work to unwind before dinner? Or do you crave a weekend morning entirely to yourself?
- **Be Consistent:** Once your boundaries are established, stick to them. Consistency demonstrates the importance of your alone time and helps your loved ones adjust their expectations.
- **Offer Alternatives:** To ease the transition, suggest alternative ways to spend time together that respect your need for solitude. Maybe it's a shared activity you enjoy in comfortable silence, like reading side-by-side or walking in nature.
- **Communicate During Planning:** When making plans with loved ones, be upfront about

your need for solitude. Suggest activities that allow for some built-in alone time or propose splitting up a longer outing with some solo time in between.

- **Be Flexible:** While consistency is important, there will be times when you might need to adjust your boundaries. Maybe a special occasion or your loved one's needs require some compromise. Be open to finding a solution that works for everyone while still prioritizing your well-being in the long run.

Setting healthy boundaries feels uncomfortable initially. However, it's crucial for establishing mutual respect and ensuring your needs are met within your relationships. Remember, prioritizing your well-being strengthens you as a partner, friend, or family member in the long run.

Finding Common Ground: Quality Time with Respect for Individual Needs

While you crave solitude, your partner or loved ones might have a stronger desire for social interaction. Here's how to find common ground:

- **Schedule Shared Activities:** Plan activities you enjoy, such as a weekend hike, movie night in, or a cooking class together. Schedule these activities and ensure they align with your social interaction preferences. Some couples might enjoy attending a sporting event or a concert, while others might find fulfillment in quieter activities like reading side-by-side or visiting a museum.

- **Respect Each Other's Needs:** Open communication is key. Discuss your individual needs for solitude and social interaction. Perhaps you need a solo morning routine, while your partner prefers an evening dedicated to connecting. Finding a schedule that respects both needs fosters a sense of understanding and strengthens your bond.

- **Quality Over Quantity:** Focus on creating meaningful connections during your shared time. Avoid distractions, be present in the moment, and actively listen to each other. This quality time spent together will be more enriching than feeling obligated to spend every moment side-by-side.

- **Embrace Spontaneity:** Leave room for unplanned moments of connection. Surprise your partner with a small gesture of affection, or take advantage of an unexpected opportunity to enjoy an activity together. These spontaneous moments of connection strengthen your bond and demonstrate that you value spending time together, even outside of scheduled activities.

- **Consider Parallel Play:** Sometimes, enjoying separate activities in the same space is fulfilling. That might look like reading different books on the couch or working on individual hobbies in a shared workspace. Parallel play allows you to enjoy each other's company while still fulfilling your individual needs for solitude and focused activity.

- **Be Flexible:** Life is unpredictable, and your schedule might need to adjust accordingly. Be open to rescheduling planned activities if one of you needs more time alone or if an unexpected opportunity for connection arises. This flexibility demonstrates understanding and respect for each other's needs.

Finding common ground involves compromise and collaboration. By understanding your own needs and the needs of your loved ones, you create a dynamic that fosters connection while respecting everyone's need for solitude.

Reframing "Me Time" as "We Time Later": A Recharge for Stronger Relationships

Shift the perspective on solitude. Instead of viewing it as time away from loved ones, frame it as a necessary "recharge" that allows you to show up in your relationships with greater energy and enthusiasm.

- **Explain the Recharge Analogy:** Explain to your loved ones that just like a phone battery needs to be recharged to function optimally, you need time alone to recharge emotionally and mentally.

- **Highlight the Benefits:** Emphasize how spending time alone allows you to manage stress, cultivate your interests, and ultimately become a more present and engaged partner or friend.

- **Focus on Quality Over Quantity:** Reassure your loved ones that while you might need some alone time, the quality of time you spend together will be more meaningful and fulfilling because you'll be coming from a place of emotional well-being.

Reframing solitude as a positive investment in your relationships alleviates any guilt or anxiety associated with needing time alone.

Appreciating Different Needs: Embracing Variations in Social Needs

It is also important to acknowledge that people have different baselines for social interaction. Your partner or friends might be extroverts who crave constant engagement, while you're an introvert who needs regular solitude.

- **Understanding Your Partner:** Recognize that your partner or loved one might have a different baseline need for social interaction than you. Some people are naturally extroverted and crave constant social engagement, while others are introverts who thrive with more alone time.

- **Open Communication Is Key:** Discuss these differences openly and honestly. Maybe your partner enjoys spending weekends socializing with friends, while you prefer solo activities like reading or spending time in nature. Communication allows you to find a balance that respects both your needs.

- **Finding Common Activities:** Look for activities that balance social interaction and solitude. Consider activities that allow for both conversation and quiet time, such as going for a walk or visiting a museum where you explore independently before coming together to discuss your experiences.

- **Respect for Boundaries:** Even if your social needs differ, respecting each other's boundaries is crucial. If your partner needs a night out with friends, support their need for social interaction. Likewise, respect your need for solitude without feeling pressured to constantly socialize.

- **Celebrating Differences:** View your differing needs for social interaction as strengths, not weaknesses. Your partner's extroversion might bring excitement and new experiences into your life, while your introversion provides a sense of calm and stability. Embrace these differences and find ways to learn from each other.

By appreciating that people have varying needs for social interaction, you build stronger, more understanding relationships. Open communication, compromise, and respect for boundaries are key to navigating these differences and finding a balance that works for both of you.

Communicating your need for solitude to loved ones is challenging, but with honesty, empathy, and a willingness to compromise, you foster understanding and build stronger, more fulfilling relationships. Solitude isn't about withdrawing from others but creating space for personal growth, ultimately allowing you to show up in your relationships with greater authenticity and emotional intelligence.

Building Stronger Connections Through Independence

Embracing solitude might seem counterintuitive to fostering strong relationships. However, the paradox lies in the fact that solitude enhances your ability to connect with others on a deeper level. By cultivating a sense of independence and self-awareness through solitude, you become a more present, engaged, and emotionally intelligent partner, friend, or family member. Here's how:

The Paradox of Connection: How Solitude Strengthens Relationships

Solitude allows you to develop a strong sense of independence. This self-reliance leads to more authentic and fulfilling connections with others.

- **Focus on Intrinsic Values:** Spending time alone allows you to explore your interests, values, and passions. This self-discovery fosters a sense of personal identity that isn't dependent on the approval of others. As a result, you connect with others based on shared genuine interests and values rather than needing external validation.

- **Reduced Need for Clinging:** When you feel secure and fulfilled within yourself, the need for constant validation or approval from others diminishes. This allows you to approach relationships with openness and emotional security, fostering healthier connections. Consider yourself in a relationship where you don't cling to your partner for your sense of identity or happiness. This newfound independence allows you to appreciate and value your partner for who they are, creating a stronger foundation for love and respect.

- **Space for Personal Growth:** Solitude provides a platform for self-reflection and personal growth. By processing your emotions and working on your self-improvement goals during alone time, you become a more well-rounded and emotionally mature individual. This personal growth translates into stronger and more meaningful relationships. If you're constantly focused on your unresolved issues, you have less emotional bandwidth to invest in truly understanding and supporting your loved ones. Solitude allows you to address your baggage, becoming a more supportive and present partner in the process.

Solitude allows you to cultivate the emotional intelligence and self-awareness necessary for building stronger, more authentic connections.

Quality Over Quantity: Prioritizing Meaningful Interactions

Solitude allows you to step back and evaluate your social circle. Here's how:

- **Identifying Unfulfilling Relationships:** Spending time alone helps you identify relationships that are draining or no longer serve you well.

This self-awareness allows you to prioritize your energy towards fostering deeper connections with those who truly enrich your life. When you're feeling centered and fulfilled from your solitude practice, you're more likely to seek out genuine conversations and connect with people on a deeper level. On the other hand, if you're feeling drained from a lack of solitude, you might find yourself resorting to superficial interactions to fill a void.

- **Appreciating Meaningful Connections:** By taking a break from constant social interaction, you gain a renewed appreciation for the truly meaningful relationships in your life. This appreciation motivates you to invest time and effort into nurturing these connections. Think about a time you went on a long vacation and how excited you were to see your loved ones upon your return. Solitude has a similar effect, reminding you of the importance of the close relationships you've cultivated.

- **Setting Boundaries:** Solitude empowers you to set healthy boundaries within your relationships. You become more comfortable prioritizing quality interactions over superficial connections, leading to a more fulfilling social life. Suppose you're attending an event where you know there will be people who drain your energy. By embracing solitude, you feel more empowered to politely excuse yourself and prioritize activities that nourish you rather than feeling obligated to stay in situations that leave you feeling depleted.

Focus on cultivating a few deep and meaningful connections rather than a large circle of shallow acquaintances. This shift in perspective, fostered by solitude, allows you to build stronger and more supportive relationships.

Being Present and Engaged: Showing Up Fully in Your Relationships

Solitude enhances your ability to be present and engaged in your interactions with others.

- **Reduced Mental Clutter:** Spending time alone allows you to clear your mind and de-stress. This mental clarity allows you to be more present and attentive during your interactions with loved ones. When having a conversation with a friend after a long day filled with back-to-back meetings, you might be mentally scattered and less engaged in the conversation. Solitude allows you to clear your headspace and truly focus on the person in front of you.

- **Active Listening:** When your mind is free from distractions, you truly listen to and understand your partner or friend. This active listening fosters a sense of connection and strengthens your bond. Think about the last time someone gave you their undivided attention. It likely felt validating and deepened your connection with that person. By embracing solitude and reducing mental clutter, you become a more effective listener, fostering stronger emotional connections with those around you.

- **Enhanced Empathy:** Solitude allows you to process your own emotions and develop a deeper understanding of your inner world. This introspection fosters empathy, allowing you to better understand and connect with the emotions of others. If you're constantly overwhelmed with your own emotions, you might have less capacity to be empathetic and supportive towards a friend going through a tough time. Solitude allows you to process your emotional baggage, creating space for empathy and compassion towards others.

Solitude reduces mental clutter, promotes active listening, and enhances empathy. It equips you to be more present and engaged in your relationships, leading to deeper connections with loved ones.

11. Actively listen to your people. Source: https://www.pexels.com/photo/multiracial-friends-drinking-coffee-in-cafe-7388889/

Bringing Your Best Self: Cultivating Emotional Intelligence through Solitude

Solitude provides a space for self-reflection and emotional processing, ultimately allowing you to bring your best self to your relationships.

- **Identifying Unhealthy Patterns:** Spending time alone allows you to identify unhealthy patterns in your thoughts and behaviors. This self-awareness empowers you to address these issues and develop healthier coping mechanisms. Suppose you're in a relationship where you tend to react impulsively when frustrated. In that case, solitude allows you to reflect on these triggers and develop strategies for managing your emotions more effectively. Bringing a more emotionally intelligent version of yourself to your relationships helps you navigate conflict with greater maturity and strengthen your bonds.

- **Setting Healthy Boundaries:** Solitude empowers you to set healthy boundaries within your relationships. By understanding your own needs and triggers, you communicate them effectively and avoid situations that drain your emotional energy. When you constantly feel pressured to do things that leave you feeling drained, solitude allows you to identify these situations and communicate your boundaries assertively, fostering healthier and more respectful relationships.

- **Personal Growth:** Solitude is a catalyst for personal growth. Processing your emotions, working on your goals, and developing a strong sense of self make you a more well-rounded individual. This personal growth spills over into your relationships, making you a more supportive, understanding, and reliable partner or friend.

Running away from your problems will never be the answer. Solitude helps you create a space for self-reflection and emotional growth. Addressing your emotional baggage and developing healthier behavioral patterns brings your best self to your relationships, fostering deeper connections and greater fulfillment.

Gratitude for Loved Ones: Appreciating the People in Your Life

Solitude also cultivates a deeper appreciation for the loved ones in your life.

- **A Renewed Perspective:** Taking a break from constant social interaction allows you to appreciate the value of meaningful connections. When you're constantly bombarded with social media updates and feeling overwhelmed by the busyness of life, solitude allows you to step back and appreciate the simple joys of spending time with loved ones, fostering a sense of gratitude for their presence in your life.

- **Quality Time Takes Intentionality:** Solitude highlights the importance of intentional interactions with loved ones. When you're not constantly surrounded by people, you become more aware of the importance of scheduling quality time with those who matter most. Think about how much more meaningful a dedicated game night with friends becomes when compared to spending every evening surrounded by acquaintances. Solitude creates a space for intentionality, fostering stronger bonds with loved ones.

- **Expressing Appreciation:** The appreciation you cultivate for your loved ones during solitude translates into expressing your gratitude more openly. Taking the time to express your appreciation for someone strengthens your bond and fosters a sense of mutual respect and care.

Solitude allows you to appreciate the importance of the close relationships in your life. By expressing your gratitude and nurturing these connections with intentionality, you build stronger and more fulfilling bonds with your loved ones.

Balancing Social Interactions with Solitary Activities

Finding a healthy balance between social interaction and solitude is key to reaping both benefits. Here's how to create a fulfilling life that incorporates your need for connection and your desire for alone time:

Creating a Schedule: Integrating Solitude into Your Week

The first step is creating a balanced schedule that incorporates both social interaction and solitude.

- **Identify Your Needs:** Reflect on your individual needs for social interaction and solitude.

How much alone time do you truly need to feel energized? How much social interaction leaves you feeling fulfilled? Be honest with yourself and use this self-awareness to create a realistic schedule.

- **Block Time for Solitude:** Treat solitude like any other important appointment. Schedule dedicated blocks of time in your calendar for solo activities, whether it's an hour of reading each morning, a solo hike over the weekend, or an evening dedicated to journaling and reflection.

- **Plan Social Activities:** Schedule time for social activities you genuinely enjoy, whether it's catching up with friends, attending a family gathering, or joining a club meeting. Ensure these activities align with your social needs and leave you feeling energized, not drained.

- **Be Flexible:** Life is unpredictable, and your schedule might need to adjust accordingly. Be open to rescheduling activities or incorporating spontaneous moments of connection, but strive to maintain a general balance between social interaction and solitude.

Creating a schedule that incorporates both your social and solitary needs provides structure and ensures you prioritize both aspects of a fulfilling life.

Saying No More Often: Setting Boundaries for Your Alone Time

Setting boundaries is crucial for maintaining a healthy balance between social interaction and solitude.

- **Prioritize Your Needs:** Remember, it's perfectly okay to say no to invitations when you need time alone. Don't feel obligated to attend every event or constantly be available. Prioritize your need for solitude and recharge time.

- **Communicate Clearly:** Be upfront and honest when you decline an invitation. You don't need to go into elaborate explanations. A simple "Thank you for the invitation, but I need some time alone this weekend" is perfectly acceptable.

- **Offer Alternatives:** If you value the relationship but need some alone time, consider suggesting an alternative activity for another time. Maybe you can reschedule for when you have more energy to interact with people.

- **Don't Feel Guilty:** Prioritizing your need for solitude isn't selfish. It's necessary for your mental and emotional well-being. Saying no to social invitations allows you to show up for the activities you truly enjoy with greater presence and enthusiasm.

Setting boundaries and saying no more often empowers you to prioritize your solitude and create a balanced life.

Learning to Recharge: Solitude as a Tool for Social Energy

Solitude doesn't mean avoiding social interaction. It's a tool for replenishing your energy for social activities.

- **Your Social Battery:** Your social energy has a battery. Constant interaction drains your battery, while solitude acts as a charger. By scheduling time alone, you allow yourself to recharge and return to social situations feeling more engaged and enthusiastic.

- **Improved Social Interactions:** When you feel rested and centered from solitude, you're more present and engaged in social interactions. You listen more attentively, participate more actively, and foster deeper connections with others.

- **Quality Over Quantity:** Prioritizing solitude allows you to focus on quality interactions over superficial connections. During your social time, you'll have more energy for meaningful conversations and activities with loved ones.

View solitude as a necessary investment in your social life. By ensuring you have enough alone time to recharge, you'll show up for social interactions with greater energy and enthusiasm, ultimately leading to more fulfilling connections.

Finding Activities You Enjoy Alone: Exploring Your Passions in Solitude

Embrace solitude as an opportunity to explore your interests and hobbies.

- **Discover New Passions:** Solitude allows you the time and space to explore new activities that pique your curiosity. Maybe you've always wanted to try meditation, learn a new language, or explore a specific genre of literature. Solitude provides the perfect environment for self-discovery and personal growth.

- **Revisit Old Hobbies:** Perhaps you have neglected hobbies you once enjoyed due to a busy social life. Solitude allows you to revisit these activities and rediscover the joy they bring you. Did you use to enjoy woodworking? Maybe playing the guitar or sketching? Solitude allows you to reconnect with these parts of yourself and rediscover the fulfillment they bring.

- **Embrace Creativity:** Solitude is a breeding ground for creativity. Use your alone time to write, paint, play music, or engage in any other creative pursuit that sparks your interest. When you're free from distractions and external influences, you tap into your inner world and explore your creative potential.

12. Embrace creativity. Source: https://www.pexels.com/photo/man-in-button-down-shirt-painting-on-a-canvas-6184414/

By identifying activities you enjoy in solitude, you create a sense of anticipation and fulfillment around your alone time. This makes solitude less about avoiding social interaction and more about embracing personal growth, exploration, and self-discovery.

Embracing Spontaneity: Leaving Room for Unexpected Connections

While prioritizing solitude is important, maintaining some flexibility for spontaneous social interaction is also enriching.

- **Leave Room for Surprise:** Don't become so rigid with your schedule that you miss out on unexpected opportunities for connection. If a close friend calls and invites you to join them for an evening event, consider joining them even if it wasn't on your initial schedule.

- **Last-Minute Recharge:** A short social interaction might be exactly what you need to recharge after a long period of solitude. A quick coffee date with a friend or a walk in the park with a neighbor provides a refreshing change of pace and a welcome dose of social interaction.

- **Maintaining Social Connections:** Occasional spontaneous interactions help maintain your social connections. Being open to these opportunities shows your loved ones that you value them and are still interested in connecting, even when prioritizing solitude.

Remember, solitude isn't about complete isolation. Leaving room for occasional unplanned social interactions adds a layer of richness and spontaneity to your life.

Finding a healthy balance between social interaction and solitude is an ongoing process. By creating a schedule, setting boundaries, and identifying activities you enjoy alone, you create a fulfilling life that incorporates the benefits of both worlds. Solitude isn't a luxury. It is necessary for emotional well-being, personal growth, and stronger and more meaningful relationships.

Throughout this chapter, you've explored the surprising ways solitude enhances your relationships. From fostering healthy communication and independence to creating a space for personal growth, the benefits of embracing solitude ripple outward, enriching your connections with loved ones.

Solitude is a journey of self-discovery that allows you to show up in your relationships with greater authenticity, emotional intelligence, and a renewed sense of purpose. By effectively communicating your need for solitude, embracing your independence, and finding a healthy balance between social interaction and solitary time, you cultivate a life rich in both meaningful connections and personal growth.

In the next chapter, you'll learn how to transform these insights into action with practical strategies for incorporating solitude into your daily routine and reaping its transformative benefits across all aspects of your life.

Chapter 5: Harnessing Creativity and Productivity

Have you ever felt a surge of inspiration strike during a quiet walk in nature or experienced a renewed sense of focus after a mindful meditation session? This chapter uncovers the surprising link between solitude and your ability to be both creative and productive. You will explore how embracing solitude acts as a catalyst for sparking new ideas, enhancing concentration, and ultimately achieving your personal and professional goals.

Whether you're a struggling artist, an overwhelmed entrepreneur, or simply someone seeking to optimize your workflow, this chapter offers practical strategies for leveraging solitude to unlock your full creative and productive potential. Get ready to discover how strategically incorporating alone time into your routine transforms you from feeling scattered and uninspired to a wellspring of innovative ideas and focused determination.

13. *Unlock your full creative and productive potential. Source: https://www.pexels.com/photo/man-in-white-crew-neck-t-shirt-holding-white-figurine-1094871/*

Finding Inspiration in Solitude

Solitude allows you to take a break from the busyness of life. It facilitates a space where your creativity flourishes. Here's how embracing solitude acts as a catalyst for generating new ideas and igniting your creative spark:

Escaping Distractions: Quieting the Noise to Amplify Your Ideas

In this fast-paced, technology-driven world, constant distractions hinder your ability to think deeply and generate original ideas. Solitude provides a refuge from this noise, allowing you to focus your mental energy and tap into your creative potential.

- **Reduced Information Overload:** Constant notifications, emails, and social media updates overwhelm your mind and hinder your ability to focus. Solitude allows you to escape this information overload, creating a clear mental space for creative thought. Compare yourself trying to write a complex scientific paper in a bustling coffee shop versus sitting alone in a quiet library. The solitude allows you to dive deeper into your research, analyze complex concepts, and synthesize information in a way that might be impossible in a distracting environment.

- **Deeper Thinking:** Without distractions, you dive deeper into your thoughts and explore ideas more fully. This allows for a more nuanced understanding of concepts and the identification of unexpected connections that spark innovation. When a musician composes a symphony, the solitude allows them to experiment with different melodies, harmonies, and rhythms, fostering a deeper exploration of the musical idea and ultimately leading to a more creative and cohesive composition.

- **Problem-Solving from Different Angles:** Solitude allows you to approach problems from different angles without the influence of external opinions. This freethinking environment fosters creative solutions and innovative approaches. Suppose you're an entrepreneur brainstorming new product ideas. By removing yourself from the influence of market trends and competitor analysis, you explore unconventional solutions and disruptive concepts that might not have emerged in a collaborative brainstorming session.

Connecting with Nature: Finding Inspiration in the Natural World

Nature has long been a source of inspiration for artists, writers, and innovators throughout history. Spending time in solitude amidst nature is a powerful catalyst for sparking creativity.

- **A Change of Scenery:** Stepping away from your usual environment shifts your perspective and sparks new ideas. Immersing yourself in nature provides a fresh visual and sensory experience that jolts your creativity out of a rut. When a painter is stuck in a creative block, a solitary hike through a vibrant forest exposes them to a kaleidoscope of colors, textures, and natural forms, igniting inspiration for a new series of paintings.

- **Beauty and Tranquility:** The beauty and tranquility of nature have a calming effect on the mind. This sense of peace allows you to detach from anxieties and enter a more receptive state, open to new ideas and creative inspiration. If you're a poet seeking inspiration for a new piece, sitting alone on a quiet beach, surrounded by the calming sounds of the waves, will allow you to connect with your emotions and tap into a deeper well of creativity.

- **Reconnecting with Your Senses:** Solitude in nature allows you to reconnect with your senses. The sights, sounds, smells, and textures of the natural world trigger unexpected associations and spark new creative directions. If a fashion designer is feeling uninspired by current trends, spending time alone in a garden will expose them to a variety of colors, textures, and intricate patterns in nature. It will inspire them to create a new clothing line that breaks away from conventional styles.

Nature provides a constant source of inspiration for those who want to embrace solitude. By quieting the external noise and immersing yourself in the natural world, you open yourself up to countless creative possibilities.

Embracing Daydreaming and Mind-Wandering: Allowing Your Imagination to Run Wild

While structured brainstorming sessions have their place, some of the most innovative ideas emerge from periods of unstructured thinking. Solitude allows you to embrace daydreaming and mind-wandering, which is a powerful source of creative inspiration.

- **Unleashing the Subconscious:** When your mind isn't focused on a specific task, it allows your subconscious to come to the forefront. This leads to unexpected connections and the emergence of ideas that might not have surfaced during focused thinking. Taking a solitary walk in nature allows your subconscious to process the information freely, leading to a sudden flash of insight that cracks any code.

- **Breaking Creative Blocks:** Feeling stuck in a creative rut? Solitude will help you break free. By allowing your mind to wander freely, you might stumble upon a new perspective or unexpected association that leads you out of your creative block. If a novelist is struggling to write the next chapter of their book, spending time alone journaling their thoughts and free-writing allows them to explore different narrative threads and character motivations. It will ultimately lead to a breakthrough in the plot.

- **Fueling Innovation:** Daydreaming and mind-wandering are the seeds of innovation. By allowing your mind to explore unconventional pathways and unexpected connections, you open yourself up to the possibility of groundbreaking ideas. If an architect is feeling uninspired by traditional building designs, spending time alone sketching and doodling will allow them to explore unconventional shapes and spatial arrangements, leading to a revolutionary new architectural concept.

Embrace solitude as a time to indulge in daydreams and free thinking. By allowing your mind to wander freely, you create fertile ground for unexpected ideas and potentially groundbreaking innovations to emerge.

Consuming Inspiring Content: Feeding Your Creativity During Solitude

Solitude doesn't have to be completely devoid of external input. Use this time to immerse yourself in inspiring content that sparks new ideas and fuels your creative fire.

- **Books and Articles:** Delving into well-written books and articles on topics that pique your interest exposes you to new perspectives and ways of thinking. This exposure sparks new ideas and ignites your creative spark. If you're a filmmaker feeling uninspired by current movies, spending time alone reading classic novels and biographies of innovative directors will expose you to diverse storytelling techniques and character development, inspiring you to create a film with a unique perspective.

- **Art and Music:** Surround yourself with art, music, and other creative expressions that resonate with you. Immersing yourself in these forms of beauty triggers new ideas and emotions, fostering a fertile ground for your creative endeavors. If you're a dancer feeling uninspired by your current routine, spending time alone listening to a variety of music and watching captivating dance performances will allow you to discover new movements and emotional expressions, inspiring you to create a groundbreaking new dance piece.

- **Museums and Galleries:** Visiting museums and galleries exposes you to a variety of artistic styles and creative expressions. Immersing yourself in these exhibits sparks new ideas and ignites your creative spirit. If you're a fashion designer feeling uninspired by current trends, exploring a museum's fashion exhibit will allow you to see how different cultures and historical periods approached clothing design, inspiring you to create a new clothing line that breaks away from conventional styles.

Solitude doesn't mean isolating yourself from all external input. Use this time to curate a personalized experience by consuming inspiring content that fuels your creative fire and sparks new ideas.

14. Visiting museums and galleries exposes you to a variety of artistic styles and creative expressions. Source: https://www.pexels.com/photo/man-standing-in-front-of-paintings-375882/

Experimentation and Exploration: The Freedom to Fail Without Judgment

Solitude provides a safe space to experiment with new ideas and approaches without fear of judgment. This freedom to fail allows you to explore uncharted creative territory and potentially stumble upon groundbreaking discoveries.

- **Trying New Things:** Solitude allows you to step outside your comfort zone and try new things without the pressure of external expectations. This experimentation leads to unexpected discoveries and innovative solutions. If you're a musician feeling uninspired by your current instrument, experimenting with new instruments will allow you to discover new sounds and musical possibilities, potentially leading to the creation of a completely new genre of music.

- **Learning from Mistakes:** The freedom to fail in solitude allows you to learn from your mistakes without fear of public scrutiny. This trial-and-error process is crucial for creative growth and innovation. If you're a scientist conducting a complex experiment, working alone in the lab will allow you to experiment with different approaches and learn from your failures without the pressure of justifying your actions to a team.

- **Developing Your Unique Voice:** Solitude allows you to explore your interests and develop your unique creative voice. Suppose you're a writer feeling the pressure to conform to popular writing styles. In that case, spending time alone writing freely will allow you to explore your voice and develop a distinct writing style that sets you apart from the competition.

Embrace solitude as a space for experimentation and exploration. By trying new things, learning from your mistakes, and developing your unique voice, you pave the way for groundbreaking creativity and innovation.

Enhancing Focus and Concentration

Apart from sparking creativity, solitude enhances your focus and concentration. By strategically incorporating alone time into your routine, you create a space for deep work and maximize your productivity. Here are some strategies to leverage solitude for peak focus:

Creating a Dedicated Workspace: Crafting Your Focus Zone

The environment you work in significantly impacts your ability to concentrate. Solitude allows you to create a dedicated workspace that minimizes distractions and optimizes focus.

- **Minimize Clutter:** A cluttered workspace overwhelms your senses and impedes concentration. Dedicate time during your solitude to clear your workspace, ensuring everything you need is readily available while eliminating unnecessary items that might draw your attention. Think of it like preparing a stage for a performance. By decluttering your workspace, you remove visual distractions and set the scene for a focused and productive performance.

- **Optimize for Focus:** Tailor your workspace to your specific needs. Some people thrive in a brightly lit environment, while others prefer a more subdued atmosphere. Experiment during your solitude to discover which lighting and temperature settings enhance your focus. Invest in tools that promote concentration, such as noise-canceling headphones or a comfortable chair. Consider factors like air quality and ergonomics. A well-lit, properly ventilated space with a supportive chair will significantly impact your ability to concentrate for extended periods.

- **Accessibility and Comfort:** Ensure your workspace is easily accessible during your dedicated solitude sessions. This minimizes the temptation to multitask or get sidetracked by other activities. Consider creating a dedicated "do not disturb" zone where you work uninterrupted. Ideally, this space should be separate from your usual relaxation areas to avoid conditioning your mind to associate the space with leisure rather than focused work.

Your dedicated workspace should be a haven for focus and uninterrupted productivity. Utilize solitude to create an environment that optimizes your concentration and allows you to concentrate on your work.

Developing a Routine: The Power of Habitual Focus

Creating a consistent routine for your solitary work sessions trains your mind to associate solitude with focused work.

- **Schedule Dedicated Time:** Block out dedicated time slots in your calendar for focused work sessions in solitude. Consistency is key. If possible, try to schedule these sessions at the same time each day. This predictability allows your mind and body to adjust and prepare for a period of deep concentration. Treat these sessions with the same importance as any critical meeting or appointment.

- **Minimize Transitions:** Structure your day to minimize disruptions when transitioning into your solitude session. Consider completing administrative tasks or checking emails beforehand to avoid feeling the need to multitask during your focused work time. Leaving loose ends for later introduces unnecessary mental clutter and hinders your ability to focus entirely on the task at hand during your solitude session.

- **Rituals for Focus:** Develop a pre-work ritual during your solitude session. This could include activities like light stretching, meditation, or listening to calming music. These rituals signal to your brain that it's time to enter a state of focused work. Just like athletes have pre-game routines to prime their bodies and minds for competition, creating a pre-work ritual during your solitude sessions helps your brain transition into a focused and productive state.

By establishing a routine for your solitude sessions, you train your mind and body to anticipate and optimize focus during your alone time. Consistency is key to reaping the benefits of solitude for enhanced concentration and peak productivity.

The Power of Silence: Minimizing Distractions for Maximum Focus

Solitude provides a natural environment to minimize distractions and enhance focus.

- **Eliminating External Noise:** Find a quiet space where you minimize external noise distractions. If necessary, use noise-canceling headphones or earplugs to block out unwanted sounds. Look for a space that is not only quiet but also free from visual distractions.

- **Internal Distractions:** While solitude minimizes external distractions, it's important to address internal distractions as well. Techniques like mindfulness meditation help you manage wandering thoughts and refocus your attention on the task at hand. Mindfulness practice during solitude allows you to become a better observer of your thoughts, enabling you to identify and gently redirect distractions without getting caught up in them.

- **The Power of Flow:** When distractions are minimized, you're more likely to enter a state of flow where you become completely absorbed in your work. This state of deep concentration allows you to achieve peak performance and complete tasks efficiently. In solitude, free from external interruptions and internal chatter, you truly immerse yourself in the work at hand, unlocking a sense of focused energy and accomplishment.

Solitude offers a natural environment for minimizing distractions and achieving laser-like focus. By strategically utilizing alone time, you silence external noise, manage internal distractions, and unlock the power of flow for peak productivity.

Managing Technology: Taming the Digital Beasts

Technology is a double-edged sword. While it's a great asset for productivity, it's also a major source of distraction. Here's how to leverage solitude to minimize digital distractions:

- **Silence Notifications:** Turn off notifications on your phone, computer, and any other devices you might use during your solitude session. Constant notification pings disrupt your train of thought and hinder your ability to focus. When you're writing a complex legal document, a single notification from social media pulls you out of your flow state, requiring significant mental effort to refocus and regain your train of thought.

- **Airplane Mode:** Consider putting your devices in airplane mode to eliminate the temptation to check emails, social media, or browse the internet. Remember, the goal is to create a distraction-free zone for focused work.

- **Utilize Specific Tools:** Certain technologies enhance focus during solitude. Consider using apps or website blockers to restrict access to distracting websites or social media platforms during your work sessions. Utilize tools like time trackers or productivity timers to structure your work and stay on task.

Technology is a valuable asset, but it's crucial to manage it effectively during solitude. By silencing notifications, considering airplane mode, and using specific focus-enhancing tools, you harness the power of technology to support your productivity in solitude.

Mindfulness Techniques: Training Your Mind for Focus

Mindfulness practices are powerful tools for enhancing concentration and focus during solitude.

- **Meditation:** Meditation helps train your mind to become a better observer of your thoughts and emotions. By practicing mindfulness meditation during your solitude sessions, you learn to identify and gently redirect distractions without getting caught up in them. If you're working on a complex design project, a few minutes of mindful breathing during your solitude session will allow you to clear your head, refocus your attention, and approach the design challenge with renewed clarity and concentration.

- **Deep Breathing Exercises:** Simple deep breathing exercises are a quick and effective way to refocus your attention and improve concentration during solitude. When you feel your mind wandering, take a few minutes to focus on your breath, inhaling deeply and exhaling slowly. This simple practice helps to calm the mind and bring your attention back to the present moment.

- **The Power of the Present Moment:** Mindfulness techniques help you stay present in the moment and avoid getting caught up in worries about the past or future. This allows you to focus your mental energy on the task at hand and maximize your productivity during your solitude sessions. By anchoring yourself in the present moment, you avoid the mental chatter and distractions that hinder your focus and derail your progress.

By incorporating mindfulness practices into your solitude routine, you train your mind for focus, improve your ability to manage distractions, and ultimately achieve peak productivity during your alone time.

Achieving Personal and Professional Goals Through Solitude

Solitude brings creativity and focus to everything you do. It's also very useful for achieving your personal and professional goals. By strategically incorporating alone time into your routine, you create a space for strategic planning, self-discipline, and focused action, ultimately paving the way for success. Here's how solitude propels you toward achieving your aspirations:

Goal Setting and Planning: Charting Your Course in Solitude

Solitude provides a quiet space to reflect on your aspirations and develop a clear road map for achieving them.

- **Uninterrupted Reflection:** The constant busyness of life makes it difficult to truly connect with your inner desires and aspirations.

Solitude allows you to step away from distractions and delve deeper into what truly matters to you. Ask yourself critical questions about your goals: What do you want to achieve? Why is this important to you? What are your long-term aspirations?

- **Strategic Planning:** Once you've identified your goals, solitude allows you to develop a clear and actionable plan. Break down your goals into smaller, achievable steps. Research strategies and resources that support your journey. If you're a student with the goal of getting into a prestigious graduate program, spending time alone will allow you to research program requirements, identify your strengths and weaknesses, and develop a personalized study plan to maximize your chances of admission.

- **Visualization:** Solitude allows you to visualize your goals with greater clarity. Imagine yourself achieving your desired outcome. What does it look and feel like? Engaging in this visualization exercise during solitude solidifies your commitment and increases your motivation to take action. Think about an athlete preparing for a competition. Visualization exercises during solitude help them rehearse their movements mentally, building confidence and focus for the actual competition.

By utilizing solitude for uninterrupted reflection, strategic planning, and visualization, you chart a clear course toward achieving your personal and professional goals.

Developing Self-Discipline: Building the Muscle for Success

Achieving any goal requires self-discipline. Solitude is a wonderful medium for developing the willpower and focus necessary to stay on track.

- **Identifying Distractions:** Solitude allows you to identify the internal and external distractions that derail your progress. Are you prone to checking social media constantly? Do you struggle to resist the temptation to multitask? By reflecting on these challenges in solitude, you develop strategies to overcome them.

- **Building Habits:** Solitude provides a space to establish and solidify positive habits that support your goals. Dedicate time during your alone time to practice these habits, whether it's daily meditation, reading industry publications, or practicing a new skill. If you're a writer wishing to write a novel, your solitude allows you to establish a consistent writing routine, free from distractions, allowing you to build the habit of writing daily and steadily progressing towards your goal.

- **Resisting Temptation:** The quiet environment of solitude allows you to develop the mental fortitude to resist temptations that hinder your progress. When faced with a distraction, use your solitude to calm your mind, refocus on your goals, and recommit to your plan. Think about an entrepreneur trying to launch a new business. Solitude allows them to resist the temptation to take on side projects or get pulled in different directions, enabling them to stay focused on their core business goals.

By using solitude to identify distractions, build positive habits, and resist temptations, you cultivate the self-discipline necessary to persevere through challenges and achieve your goals.

Overcoming Procrastination: Taking Action in the Absence of Noise

Procrastination is a major roadblock to achieving goals. Solitude helps you silence the internal chatter and take decisive action.

- **Reducing Overwhelm:** The constant barrage of information and tasks in your daily life is overwhelming, leading to procrastination. Solitude allows you to step back from the noise and gain clarity on the task at hand. By simplifying your environment and focusing on a single task during your alone time, you feel more empowered to take action. If you are a student overwhelmed by a long to-do list, spending time alone will allow you to prioritize your tasks, break down complex projects into manageable steps, and feel more in control, reducing the urge to procrastinate.

- **Breaking Down Barriers:** Solitude allows you to identify the fears or anxieties that might be holding you back from taking action. Are you afraid of failure? Do you lack confidence in your abilities? Reflecting on these challenges in solitude helps you develop strategies to overcome them and move forward. Think about an artist who is hesitant to share their work with the world. Solitude allows them to explore their fears of rejection, develop strategies for building confidence, and ultimately take the leap to showcase their work publicly.

- **Focus and Flow:** Solitude minimizes distractions, allowing you to enter a state of flow where you become completely absorbed in the task at hand. This state of deep concentration allows you to make significant progress on your goals in a shorter period. If you're a programmer tackling a complex coding challenge, your solitude allows you to enter a state of flow, working with focused intensity and completing the task efficiently.

By utilizing solitude to reduce overwhelm, break down barriers, and enter a state of flow, you overcome procrastination and take consistent action toward achieving your goals.

Embracing the Power of Solitude for Action

Solitude provides an environment conducive to entering a state of flow, where you become completely absorbed in the task at hand.

- **Minimizing Distractions:** Free from external interruptions and internal chatter, solitude allows you to focus all your mental energy on the task at hand. This minimizes procrastination and allows you to make significant progress towards your goals. Your solitude eliminates distractions in a way that allows you to solve problems creatively.

- **Increased Productivity:** By eliminating distractions and promoting focused action, solitude allows you to maximize your productivity during dedicated work sessions. This focused work allows you to accomplish more in a shorter amount of time, propelling you closer to achieving your goals. For a salesperson working on a critical proposal, their solitude allows them to research, write, and edit the proposal with laser focus, ensuring a high-quality document that increases their chances of closing the deal.

By leveraging solitude to reduce overwhelm, break down barriers, and enter a state of focused action, you overcome procrastination and make significant strides toward achieving your goals.

15. Increase your productivity. Source: https://www.pexels.com/photo/man-in-black-long-sleeve-shirt-sitting-at-table-4064828/

Embracing Discomfort and Challenge: Stepping Outside Your Comfort Zone in Solitude

Growth often lies outside your comfort zone. Solitude is a safe space to push yourself beyond your perceived limitations.

- **Confronting Self-Doubt:** Solitude allows you to confront self-doubt and limiting beliefs that might be holding you back. Are you afraid of taking risks? Do you underestimate your capabilities? By acknowledging these challenges, you develop strategies to overcome them and embrace new opportunities. Suppose you're an athlete training for a challenging competition. In that case, solitude allows you to confront your anxieties about performance, visualize success, and develop a mental game plan for overcoming obstacles during the competition.

- **Experimentation and Iteration:** Solitude provides a safe space to experiment with new approaches and learn from your mistakes. Free from the judgment of others, you try new things, fail without consequence, and iterate on your ideas. Suppose you're an entrepreneur developing a new product. In that case, your solitude allows you to experiment with different prototypes, gather feedback from trusted advisors during limited solo consultations, and refine your product based on their learnings before launching it publicly.

- **Building Resilience:** By stepping outside your comfort zone in solitude, you develop resilience and the mental fortitude to navigate challenges and setbacks. If you're a writer facing rejection from a publisher, solitude allows you to process your disappointment, learn from the feedback, and come back stronger and more determined to succeed.

By using solitude to confront self-doubt, experiment with new approaches, and build resilience, you embrace challenges, unlock your full potential, and achieve goals that might have once seemed out of reach.

Celebrating Achievements: Reflecting on Progress in Solitude

When you're too caught up in striving for goals, solitude compels you to acknowledge your accomplishments.

- **Taking Stock of Progress:** Solitude provides a space for quiet reflection on your progress. Have you achieved any milestones lately? How far have you come on your journey? Taking time during solitude to celebrate your victories, regardless of how small, boosts your motivation and keeps you moving forward. If you're a student who just completed a challenging semester, spending time alone will allow you to reflect on your hard work, celebrate your achievements, and recharge before tackling the next challenge.

- **Renewing Commitment:** Solitude allows you to reaffirm your commitment to your goals. Why are these goals important to you? What motivates you to keep going? Reflecting on these questions during your alone time reignites your passion and refocuses your energy. Think about an activist working towards social change. Solitude allows them to reconnect with their core values, celebrate their progress, and recommit to their mission for long-term success.

- **Gratitude and Appreciation:** Solitude allows you to cultivate gratitude for the resources and support that have helped you on your journey. Taking time to appreciate your progress and the people who have helped you along the way boosts your morale and fuels your motivation to keep striving for your goals. If you're an artist who just had your first successful exhibition, spending time alone will allow you to express gratitude for your talent, the support of your loved ones, and the opportunities that led to your success.

By incorporating moments of reflection and celebration into your solitude routine, you acknowledge your accomplishments, renew your commitment to your goals, and cultivate a sense of gratitude that fuels your motivation for continued success.

Throughout this chapter, you've explored the transformative power of solitude on creativity and productivity. From fostering a fertile ground for new ideas to enhancing your ability to focus and execute, embracing solitude extends far beyond simply taking a break.

Solitude isn't about withdrawing from the world. It lets you create the space necessary to tap into your inner wellspring of creativity and focus. By incorporating these strategies into your life, you transform periods of solitude from moments of downtime into a catalyst for peak performance, allowing you to achieve your goals and live a life brimming with innovation and productivity.

In the next chapter, you'll explore the practical aspects of incorporating solitude into your daily routine. You'll explore techniques for creating a dedicated solitude space, overcoming social anxieties, and scheduling your time for maximum impact.

Chapter 6: Cultivating Inner Strength

Life throws curveballs. Unforeseen challenges, setbacks, and moments of doubt can leave you vulnerable and lost. However, within you lies a wellspring of inner strength waiting to be tapped. This chapter delves into the essential practices for cultivating unwavering resilience and self-confidence. You'll explore how embracing vulnerability can paradoxically make you stronger and how solitude is a powerful tool for discovering your purpose and forging a rock-solid sense of identity.

16. Cultivate inner strength. Source: Designed by Freepik. https://www.freepik.com/free-photo/full-shot-man-meditating-rock-h_34877579.htm

Whether you're facing a personal challenge, navigating a professional hurdle, or simply seeking to build a more robust inner foundation, this chapter equips you with practical strategies. By incorporating these practices into your daily life, you'll transform yourself from being fragile and reactive to challenges into a person who embodies unwavering strength, resilience, and unwavering self-belief.

Building Self-Confidence and Resilience

Self-confidence and resilience are the cornerstones of inner strength. This section explores how solitude assists you in cultivating these essential qualities.

Facing Your Fears: Confronting Challenges in Solitude

Solitude provides a safe space to confront your fears and anxieties head-on. You can build self-confidence and resilience by overcoming challenges in a controlled environment.

- **Identify Your Fears:** The first step is identifying what scares you. What challenges hold you back? Are you afraid of public speaking? Do you fear failure? Take time to write down your fears and anxieties, unearthing the root causes of your apprehension.

- **Develop a Challenge Plan:** Once you've identified your fears, create a plan for gradually exposing yourself to them in a safe, controlled environment. Solitude allows you to practice facing your fears without external pressure. For example, if you're afraid of public speaking, practice your presentation alone in front of a mirror or record yourself delivering it and watch it back privately. As you progress, consider joining a local public speaking group where you can practice in a supportive environment and receive constructive feedback.

- **Celebrate Small Victories:** As you overcome your challenges, no matter how small, take time to celebrate your victories. This positive reinforcement strengthens your self-belief and motivates you to continue facing your fears. Reflect on your progress during your solitude, acknowledging how far you've come and the courage you've demonstrated. Did you stammer a little during your first practice presentation? Celebrate that you got through it. This reinforcement loop builds confidence as you chip away at your fears.

By following these steps, you can use solitude to transform fear into self-confidence.

Embracing Imperfections: Self-Acceptance and Learning from Mistakes

The pursuit of perfection is a significant roadblock to building self-confidence. Solitude allows for self-reflection and fosters the acceptance of imperfections.

- **Reflect on Mistakes:** Solitude provides a quiet space to reflect on your mistakes and setbacks. Journaling during your alone time allows you to analyze your actions and identify areas for improvement. However, avoid dwelling on negativity. Instead, focus on what you learned from the experience. Ask yourself questions like "What could I have done differently?" or "What can I take away from this situation?"

- **Practice Self-Compassion:** Treat yourself with kindness and understanding when you make mistakes. Solitude empowers you to develop a more compassionate inner voice. For example, if you're talking to a close friend who made a similar mistake, what words of encouragement and support would you offer them? Extend that same kindness and understanding to yourself during your solitude.

- **Reframing Failure:** View setbacks as learning opportunities rather than failures. Solitude empowers you to reframe your perspective and identify the valuable lessons gleaned from your mistakes. Think about an athlete who misses a game-winning shot. Solitude empowers them to analyze the play, identify areas for improvement in their technique or mental approach, and use this experience to become a stronger player in the future.

By embracing imperfections and learning from mistakes in solitude, you can cultivate self-acceptance and build resilience. The key is to shift your mindset from "I blew it" to "I learned from it," fostering a growth mindset that enables you to bounce back from setbacks stronger than before.

Developing a Growth Mindset: Challenges as Opportunities for Growth

The way you view challenges significantly impacts your self-confidence and resilience. Solitude allows you to cultivate a growth mindset, where you see obstacles as opportunities for learning and development.

- **Challenge Negative Beliefs:** Many people hold limiting beliefs that hinder their self-confidence. Solitude empowers you to identify and challenge these negative thought patterns. For example, the belief "I'm not good enough" can be reframed as "I am always learning and growing." Journaling during your alone time can help you identify and challenge these limiting beliefs. Write down your negative thoughts and then actively dispute them with evidence of your capabilities and accomplishments.

- **Focus on Effort Over Outcome:** Focus on the effort you put into a task rather than just the outcome. This shift in perspective allows you to celebrate your progress and perseverance, regardless of the final result. Reflect on your journey during your solitude, acknowledging the hard work and dedication you invested. This will build self-confidence in your abilities. Did you spend months training for a race but not achieve your desired finishing time? Solitude enables you to acknowledge the effort you put in, the improvements you made, and the determination you displayed. These are all valuable aspects of the experience regardless of the outcome.

Building a Strong Inner Voice: Forging Your Path in Solitude

Solitude requires confronting challenges and fostering self-acceptance. It helps you forge your path and develop a strong inner voice. This inner voice is your compass, guiding you through life's complexities with unwavering self-belief and authenticity.

- **Unveiling Your Core Values:** The foundation of a strong inner voice lies in a deep understanding of your core values. What principles are fundamental to you? What kind of person do you aspire to be? Solitude provides a quiet space for introspection, free from external distractions. Journaling during your alone time is a transformative exercise. Write about situations where you felt a sense of fulfillment or accomplishment. What values were you upholding in those moments? By reflecting on these experiences, you can begin to identify the core principles that guide your decisions and actions.

- **Owning Your Beliefs:** A strong inner voice isn't afraid to express its convictions. Solitude allows you to explore your beliefs without judgment. Read books and articles on diverse topics that spark your curiosity. Engage in thoughtful conversations with people who hold different perspectives. As you discover new ideas and challenge your assumptions, your belief system will solidify. Solitude then becomes a space to refine your convictions and develop the courage to stand by them, even in the face of opposing viewpoints.

- **Setting Healthy Boundaries:** A strong inner voice empowers you to set healthy boundaries with others. Solitude empowers you to reflect on your needs and limitations. Think back to situations where you felt drained or taken advantage of. What were the underlying factors? Journaling during your alone time can help you identify unhealthy dynamics and patterns in your interactions. By understanding your needs and dealbreakers, you can establish boundaries that protect your well-being and emotional energy. This enables you to engage with the world in a way that feels authentic and aligned with your values.

- **Living with Authenticity:** Ultimately, a strong inner voice empowers you to live a life true to yourself. By reflecting on your core beliefs, setting healthy boundaries, and owning your convictions in solitude, you cultivate a deep sense of self-acceptance. This authenticity shines through in your interactions with others, fostering genuine connections and attracting people who resonate with your values. Solitude becomes a space to refine your sense of self, allowing you to express yourself authentically and with confidence in every aspect of your life.

Building a strong inner voice is an ongoing journey. Solitude provides the fertile ground where self-discovery flourishes. By embracing the quiet introspection that solitude offers, you can cultivate a sense of self-belief, unwavering in its authenticity, and become the architect of your path.

Practicing Self-Compassion: Kindness as the Cornerstone of Strength

More than toughness or stoicism, inner strength is about the ability to navigate life's challenges with kindness and understanding, especially towards yourself. Solitude provides a safe space to cultivate self-compassion, a cornerstone of resilience and self-confidence.

- **Mindful Self-Talk:** The way you talk to yourself has a profound impact on your self-esteem. Solitude allows you to observe your inner dialogue and replace negative self-talk with kind and encouraging messages. During your alone time, practice mindfulness exercises that help you become aware of your self-talk patterns. When you catch yourself using harsh language, gently redirect your thoughts and speak to yourself with the same compassion you would offer a loved one facing a similar situation.

- **Acknowledging Your Emotions:** Solitude allows you to acknowledge and validate your emotions without judgment. Trying to suppress difficult emotions can lead to stress and anxiety. During your alone time, engage in activities like journaling or meditation that allow you to explore your feelings. Write down what you're experiencing and why you might be feeling that way. Simply acknowledging your emotions is a powerful first step towards processing and releasing them.

- **Practicing Forgiveness:** Holding onto resentment is a heavy burden. Solitude enables you to forgive yourself and others for past mistakes. Journaling during your alone time is a helpful tool for letting go. Write a letter to yourself or the person you're holding resentment towards, expressing your emotions, and then practicing forgiveness. Forgiveness is a gift you give yourself, allowing you to move forward with greater emotional clarity and inner peace.

- **Celebrating Your Victories (Big and Small):** Taking time to acknowledge your accomplishments, no matter how small, reinforces a positive self-image. Solitude empowers you to savor your victories and celebrate your progress. During your alone time, reflect on the things you're proud of, big or small. Did you finally master that challenging yoga pose? Did you complete a difficult task at work? Take time to acknowledge your efforts and celebrate your achievements. This positive reinforcement strengthens your self-belief and motivates you to keep striving for excellence.

By incorporating these practices into your solitude routine, you can cultivate self-compassion, a vital component of inner strength. Being kind to yourself isn't a sign of weakness. It's the foundation for building resilience, self-confidence, and the unwavering belief in your ability to navigate life's complexities with grace and strength.

Embracing Vulnerability as a Strength

People often associate vulnerability with weakness. However, embracing vulnerability is, paradoxically, a source of immense strength. Solitude provides a safe space to explore your vulnerabilities, fostering deeper connections with yourself and others.

Reframing Vulnerability: Strength in Connection

Vulnerability isn't about spilling your secrets to everyone or baring your soul to the world. It's about allowing yourself to be seen and heard authentically, including your imperfections.

- **Challenge Your Assumptions:** Reflect on your beliefs about vulnerability. Write down the negative connotations you associate with vulnerability. Then, challenge these assumptions. Consider the strength it takes to be open and honest with others, even when it feels scary.

- **Shift Your Perspective:** View vulnerability as a bridge for connection. When you share your authentic self, you create space for others to do the same. This fosters deeper, more meaningful relationships built on trust and mutual understanding. Consider a time when you confided in a close friend about a personal struggle. Did sharing your vulnerability strengthen your bond and create a deeper sense of intimacy?

- **Practice Open Communication:** Start by practicing open communication with someone you trust. Solitude allows you to prepare for these conversations by reflecting on what you want to share and how you want to express yourself. During your interactions, express your thoughts and feelings honestly, focusing on "I" statements to avoid blame. For example, instead of saying, "You never listen to me," try, "I feel unheard when you interrupt me." This approach takes ownership of your emotions while fostering a more constructive dialogue.

By reframing vulnerability as a strength that fosters connection, you open yourself up to experiencing the richness of authentic relationships.

Expressing Your Emotions: Processing and Releasing in Solitude

Solitude provides a safe space to process and express your emotions, even the difficult ones. Suppressing your emotions can lead to emotional turmoil and hinder your ability to connect with others authentically.

- **Acknowledge Your Feelings:** The first step is acknowledging your emotions without judgment. Solitude allows you to explore your feelings in a safe space. Journaling during your alone time helps you process emotions. Write down what you're feeling and why you might be experiencing those emotions. Are you feeling anxious about an upcoming presentation? Frustrated by a recent setback? Acknowledging these feelings is the first step towards processing and releasing them.

- **Creative Expression:** Solitude enables you to explore creative outlets for expressing your emotions. Activities like painting, dancing, or playing music can provide a healthy release for difficult feelings. If you're feeling overwhelmed, try putting on some music and letting your body move freely. The physical release of movement can often help to release pent-up emotions. Experiment with different creative mediums and find what resonates with you.

- **Mindfulness Practices:** Mindfulness exercises like meditation can help you observe your emotions without getting swept away by them. Solitude allows you to practice these techniques in a quiet, distraction-free environment. Focus on your breath and observe your thoughts and feelings with a sense of detachment. As you become more mindful of your emotional state, you'll be better equipped to express your emotions authentically and healthily.

By processing and expressing your emotions in solitude, you cultivate emotional intelligence and the ability to connect with others on a deeper level. When you're comfortable with your vulnerability, you create space for others to be vulnerable with you, fostering genuine connection and empathy.

Building Trust Through Vulnerability: Deepening Relationships

Vulnerability builds trust with loved ones. Sharing your authentic self fosters, a sense of intimacy and connection.

- **Start Small:** You don't have to reveal your deepest secrets right away. Start by sharing small vulnerabilities with someone you trust. Solitude empowers you to reflect on what you feel comfortable sharing and prepare yourself for open communication. Perhaps you can confide in a friend about a fear you've been holding onto or express your appreciation for their presence in your life.

- **Active Listening:** Vulnerability is a two-way street. When someone shares their vulnerabilities with you, practice active listening. Solitude allows you to reflect on the importance of attentive listening and how you can be a safe space for others. During conversations, focus on truly understanding what the other person is saying, offering support and empathy without judgment. Put away distractions, make eye contact, and ask clarifying questions to demonstrate your genuine interest in their perspective.

- **Focus on Empathy:** When someone is vulnerable with you, strive to understand their experience from their perspective. Solitude allows you to cultivate empathy, the ability to feel what others feel. Imagine yourself in their shoes. What might they be feeling? What challenges are they facing? By developing your capacity for empathy, you create a safe space for vulnerability and deepen your connection with loved ones.

- **Validate Their Emotions:** Let the person know that their feelings are valid. Avoid dismissive comments like "It's not a big deal" or "You shouldn't feel that way." Solitude enables you to reflect on the importance of emotional validation and how to express it authentically. Instead, try phrases like "I understand why you feel that way" or "It sounds like you're going through a tough time." Simply acknowledging their emotions creates comfort and support.

By following these steps, you can leverage vulnerability to build trust and create deeper, more meaningful relationships with the people who matter most.

17. Focus on Empathy. Source: https://www.pexels.com/photo/friends-sitting-in-a-park-5543374/

Finding Strength in Authenticity: Embracing Your True Self

Vulnerability allows you to shed the masks you wear for the world and embrace your true self, imperfections, and all. This authenticity is a source of immense strength.

- **Identify Your Values:** Solitude provides a space to reflect on your core values and what truly matters to you. Write down situations where you felt like you were compromising your values. What motivated you to do so? By understanding your core principles, you can make choices that align with your authentic self.

- **Cherish Your Uniqueness:** You have unique qualities, quirks, and experiences that shape who you are. Solitude empowers you to celebrate your individuality. During your alone time, reflect on what makes you special. What are your passions? What skills and talents do you possess? Accept what makes you unique, and don't be afraid to express it authentically.

- **Set Boundaries to Protect Yourself:** While vulnerability is important, it's equally important to protect yourself from emotional harm. Solitude enables you to reflect on your boundaries and how to communicate them effectively. Journaling can help you identify situations where you feel drained or taken advantage of. What were the underlying factors? By understanding your needs and deal-breakers, you can establish boundaries that protect your well-being.

Living authentically doesn't mean sharing everything with everyone. It's about being true to yourself, expressing your values, and setting boundaries that protect your emotional space. This self-acceptance fosters a sense of inner strength and allows you to connect with others on a genuine level.

Setting Healthy Boundaries: Vulnerability with Protection

Being vulnerable doesn't mean leaving yourself emotionally exposed. Healthy boundaries are essential for protecting yourself from emotional harm while still fostering connection.

- **Identify Your Needs:** The first step is to understand your own needs and limitations. Solitude allows you to reflect on what drains your energy and what makes you feel supported. Write down situations where you felt emotionally depleted. What were the underlying factors? By understanding your needs, you can establish boundaries that protect your well-being.

- **Communicate Your Boundaries Assertively:** Once you've identified your boundaries, communicate them to others clearly and assertively. Solitude empowers you to practice these conversations beforehand, feeling confident and prepared. Use "I" statements to avoid accusations. For example, instead of saying, "You always interrupt me," try, "I feel unheard when you interrupt me. Can you please give me a chance to finish speaking?"

- **Respecting Other's Boundaries:** While it's important to establish your boundaries, it's equally important to respect the boundaries of others. Solitude enables you to reflect on the importance of reciprocity in relationships. Pay attention to verbal and nonverbal cues that someone might be uncomfortable with a certain level of vulnerability. Respect their boundaries and adjust your communication style accordingly.

By setting healthy boundaries, you create a safe space for vulnerability while protecting yourself from emotional harm. This allows you to connect with others authentically and build trusting relationships.

Finding Purpose and Identity in Solitude: Charting Your Course

Life is filled with noise and distractions, making it difficult to connect with your inner self and discover what truly matters. Solitude provides a quiet space for self-exploration, a sanctuary where you can embark on a journey of self-discovery and forge a strong sense of purpose and identity.

Connecting with Your Core Values: Unveiling Your Guiding Principles

Your core values are the fundamental beliefs that guide your decisions and actions. Identifying these values is the cornerstone of finding purpose and living authentically. Solitude allows for introspection, free from external influences.

- **Reflect on Defining Moments:** Think back to experiences that left a lasting impression on you, both positive and negative. Solitude equips you to journal about these moments. What aspects of the situation resonated with you? What did you learn about yourself from those experiences? For example, did helping others through a difficult time bring you a sense of fulfillment? This could point towards a value like compassion or service to others.

- **Analyze Your Emotional Reactions:** Pay attention to your emotional responses to situations. Solitude empowers you to explore the "why" behind your feelings. Write down situations that evoke strong emotions in you. Were you angry at a perceived injustice? Elated by achieving a goal?

Identifying the emotions and the situations that trigger them can reveal your underlying values.

- **Create a Values Statement:** Once you've identified some of your core values, solitude allows you to refine them into a concise statement. Journaling can help you articulate your values clearly. Write down your core values and what they mean to you. For example, a value like "integrity" might translate to "I strive to be honest and act with fairness in all my interactions." Having a clear understanding of your values becomes the compass that guides you toward a purposeful life.

Setting Personal Goals: Aligning Your Aspirations with Your Values

Your goals are the steppingstones on your path toward purpose. Solitude allows you to set goals that are aligned with your core values, ensuring your journey is meaningful and fulfilling.

- **Brainstorm Freely:** Solitude allows for free-flowing brainstorming without judgment. Journaling during your alone time is a great way to explore your aspirations. Write down everything you hope to achieve in life, big or small. Don't worry about practicality at this stage. Simply capture all your desires and dreams.

- **Prioritize Based on Values:** Once you have a comprehensive list of goals, use your solitude to evaluate them against your core values. Journaling can help you analyze each goal and identify the values it aligns with. Ask yourself: "Does this goal bring me closer to living a life that reflects my values?" Prioritize goals that resonate most deeply with your core principles.

- **Set SMART Goals:** Now that you have identified your most meaningful goals, solitude enables you to refine them using the SMART framework. Make your goals Specific, Measurable, Achievable, Relevant, and Time-bound. Journaling can help you translate your broad goals into actionable steps. For example, a broad goal of "being healthy" can be transformed into a SMART goal of "exercising for 30 minutes three times a week for the next three months."

By setting goals aligned with your values, you create a road map for a life filled with purpose and meaning.

Discovering Your Passions: Unearthing What Ignites Your Spark

Your passions are the activities that ignite your enthusiasm and bring you joy. Solitude provides the quiet space to reconnect with these intrinsic motivators, guiding you towards a fulfilling purpose.

- **Experiment Without Pressure:** Solitude empowers you to try new things without fear of judgment. This is a time for exploration and discovery. During your alone time, engage in activities that have always sparked your curiosity but that you might not have had the time or courage to pursue before. Take a painting class, try a new sport, or delve into a fascinating documentary.

- **Reflect on Engagement:** After trying a new activity in solitude, write about your experience in a journal. Did you lose track of time? Were you completely absorbed in the process? These are signs that you might have tapped into a passion. Pay attention to the activities that bring you a sense of fulfillment and flow.

- **Nurture Your Passions:** Once you've identified some potential passions, use your solitude to brainstorm ways to integrate them into your life. Journaling can help you develop an action plan. Can you volunteer your time with an organization related to your passion? Can you take a class to further develop your skills?

- **Nurture Your Passions:** Once you've identified some potential passions, use your solitude to brainstorm ways to integrate them into your life. Journaling can help you develop an action plan. Consider these questions:

- **Dedicate a Specific Time to Pursue Your Passion:** Even a small amount of dedicated time can make a big difference. Scheduling regular time for your passion in your solitude can help you develop your skills and keep the spark alive.

- **Find a Like-minded Community:** Solitude is a launching pad for connection. Look for online forums, local clubs, or workshops related to your passion. Connecting with others who share your interests can provide encouragement, support, and new perspectives.

- **Set Achievable Goals:** Solitude equips you to break down larger goals into manageable steps. Journaling can help you map out a clear path for progress. Setting small goals and celebrating your achievements keeps you motivated and fosters a sense of accomplishment.

By nurturing your passions in solitude, you cultivate a wellspring of joy and fulfillment, enriching your life and guiding you toward a purpose that feels authentic and deeply satisfying.

18. Ignite your inner spark. Source: https://www.pexels.com/photo/fireworks-761547/

Living a Life of Authenticity: Embracing Your True Self

Discovering your purpose involves identifying goals and passions. It's all about living a life true to yourself. Solitude provides a safe space to shed societal expectations and accept your authentic self, the foundation for a fulfilling purpose.

- **Challenge Societal Expectations:** Solitude allows you to reflect on societal pressures and expectations that might not align with your true self. Write down situations where you felt like you were conforming to external pressures. What were the underlying expectations? How did compromising your authenticity make you feel? Recognizing these societal influences empowers you to break free and live according to your values and passions.

- **Believe You're Special:** You possess unique talents, skills, and experiences that shape who you are. Solitude allows you to celebrate your individuality. Journaling during your alone time can help you identify what makes you special. Write down the strengths, quirks, and experiences that contribute to your unique perspective. Embrace what makes you different, and don't be afraid to express your authentic self in all areas of your life.

- **Prioritize Authenticity Over Approval Seeking:** The pursuit of external validation can hinder your ability to live authentically. Solitude allows you to reflect on your motivations. Write down situations where you felt compelled to act a certain way to gain approval. What was the underlying fear of rejection? By understanding your motivations, you can prioritize living according to your values, even if it means not always receiving external validation.

Living authentically allows you to radiate genuine confidence and connect with others on a deeper level. This authenticity becomes a cornerstone of a life filled with purpose and meaning.

Finding Your Place in the World: A Life Aligned with Purpose

Along with self-discovery, solitude is about using your new-found awareness to find your place in the world and contribute your unique gifts.

- **Identify Your Contribution:** Solitude empowers you to reflect on how you can use your skills, passions, and values to contribute to the world around you. Write down your strengths and talents. How can you leverage them to make a positive impact? Are you passionate about environmental issues? Perhaps you can volunteer your time with a local conservation organization.

- **Align Your Purpose with Action:** Don't wait for the "perfect" opportunity to take action. Solitude allows you to brainstorm ways to integrate your purpose into your daily life. Journaling can help you develop an action plan. Start small and focus on taking consistent steps towards a more meaningful life. Can you mentor a young person interested in your field? Can you donate a portion of your time or resources to a cause you care about?

- **Embrace Continuous Growth:** Finding your purpose is a lifelong journey of exploration and growth. Solitude provides a space for ongoing self-reflection and refinement. Journaling during your alone time allows you to track your progress, celebrate your achievements, and identify areas for further exploration. As you learn and grow, your purpose may evolve, and that's perfectly okay. Embrace the journey of continuous discovery and keep striving to live a life that aligns with your deepest values and aspirations.

By embarking on this journey of self-discovery in solitude, you'll gain the clarity and confidence to step into the world with a renewed sense of purpose. You'll be empowered to live a life that is not just successful but deeply fulfilling, contributing your unique gifts to the world, and leaving a positive impact on those around you.

Throughout this chapter, you've explored the transformative power of cultivating inner strength. From bolstering self-confidence and embracing vulnerability to discovering purpose in solitude, the practices outlined here can empower you to navigate life's complexities with grace and resilience.

Inner strength isn't about becoming invincible. It's about developing the courage to face challenges head-on, the resilience to bounce back from setbacks, and the unwavering belief in your ability to overcome anything life throws your way. As you incorporate these practices into your life, you'll cultivate a profound sense of inner strength that radiates outward, allowing you to live a life brimming with confidence, purpose, and unwavering self-belief.

Chapter 7: Embracing Solitude in Modern Life

In this hyper-connected world, the constant barrage of notifications, social media updates, and the pressure to be "always on" can leave you feeling overwhelmed and depleted. Yet, amidst this digital frenzy lies a powerful antidote: solitude. This chapter explores the transformative potential of embracing solitude in modern life. Far from being a state of isolation, solitude is a sacred space for self-discovery, rejuvenation, and the cultivation of inner strength.

19. Set time away from modern life's noise. Source: https://www.pexels.com/photo/person-holding-iphone-showing-social-networks-folder-607812/

Here, you'll discover practical tips for incorporating solitude into your daily routine, even amidst a busy schedule. You'll explore strategies for creating dedicated spaces for quiet reflection and discuss effective ways to navigate social pressures that might discourage you from embracing solitude. Whether you crave a few stolen moments of peace in the midst of the chaos or yearn for longer stretches of uninterrupted introspection, this chapter equips you with the tools and strategies to cultivate a nourishing relationship with solitude. So, put down your phone, silence the notifications, and prepare to embark on a journey of self-discovery and inner strength.

Practical Tips for Incorporating Alone Time into Daily Routine

Feeling constantly pulled in a million directions? Does the ever-present hum of technology leave you yearning for a moment of quiet reflection? Carving out dedicated time for solitude can feel like a luxury in your busy life, yet it's a vital ingredient for well-being and personal growth. This section equips you with practical strategies to seamlessly integrate solitude into your daily routine, even amidst a packed schedule.

Scheduling "Me Time": Blocking Off Sacred Time for Yourself

The first step towards embracing solitude is acknowledging its importance. Solitude is an essential appointment, just as important as a work meeting or doctor's visit. By scheduling dedicated "me time" in your calendar, you signal to yourself and others that your alone time is valuable and non-negotiable.

- **Identify Your Ideal Time Slot:** Reflect on your natural energy levels. Are you a morning person who craves quiet reflection before the day begins? Or do you find yourself yearning for solitude in the evening hours to unwind and decompress? Schedule your alone time during a period when you're most likely to be focused and uninterrupted.

- **Start Small and Be Consistent:** Don't overwhelm yourself by trying to carve out a large chunk of time right away. Begin with manageable increments, perhaps 15-30 minutes a day. Consistency is key. Scheduling regular solitude sessions, even if brief, will establish a habit and make it easier to prioritize alone time in the long run.

- **Block It Out on Your Calendar:** Treat your alone time with the same respect you would any other appointment. Block off the dedicated time slot in your calendar and share it with anyone who might need to know, such as family members or housemates. This prevents scheduling conflicts and also sends a clear message about the importance of this time for you.

- **Be Flexible When Needed:** Life happens, and unexpected events might occasionally disrupt your solitude schedule. Don't beat yourself up if you need to reschedule your alone time. The key is to recommit finding a suitable time slot within the same day or week, demonstrating your commitment to prioritizing solitude.

- **Consider "Micro-Solitude" Moments:** Even on days when a dedicated solitude session isn't feasible. You can still incorporate brief moments of quiet throughout the day. Take a solo walk during your lunch break, step outside for a few mindful breaths between tasks, or enjoy a cup of coffee in silence before the day begins. These "micro-moments" of solitude can add up and provide a much-needed mental break.

Actionable Step: Schedule your solitude session right after waking up or before bed. The quiet stillness of these liminal times is particularly conducive to introspection and self-reflection. However, if you find yourself hitting the snooze button or struggling to stay awake, experiment with a different time slot.

By following these steps, you can transform solitude from a distant aspiration into a regular part of your daily routine. Scheduling "me time" demonstrates the value you place on your well-being and sets the foundation for a more mindful and fulfilling life.

Creating a Solitude Ritual: Signaling the Start of Your Alone Time

Your brain thrives on routines and rituals. Creating a dedicated solitude ritual signals to your mind and body that it's time to shift gears and enter a state of quiet reflection. This ritual can be as simple or elaborate as you like. The key is to find practices that signal the beginning of your alone time and promote a sense of calm and focus.

- **Craft a Personalized Ritual:** Consider activities you find calming and enjoyable. Do you find lighting a scented candle creates a sense of peace? Perhaps gentle stretching or a short yoga routine helps you transition into a more mindful state. Experiment and discover what works best for you.

- **Create a Dedicated Space (Optional):** If possible, designate a specific area in your home as your solitude sanctuary. This could be a quiet corner in your bedroom, a cozy reading nook, or even a designated chair on your balcony. Having a dedicated space reinforces the association between the location and your solitude practice.

- **Engage Your Senses:** Sensory cues can powerfully enhance your solitude experience. Play calming music, light a diffuser with your favorite essential oil, or sip on a soothing herbal tea. Engaging your senses creates a multi-dimensional experience that deepens your state of relaxation and focus.

- **Minimize Distractions:** Put your phone on silent mode and turn off any notifications on your computer. The goal is to create a distraction-free environment that enables you to fully immerse yourself in your alone time.

- **Start with a Grounding Practice:** Consider incorporating a short grounding practice at the beginning of your solitude ritual. This could be a few minutes of deep breathing exercises, mindful meditation, or writing down a few things you're grateful for in a gratitude journal. Grounding practices help center your attention and prepare your mind for introspection.

Actionable Step: Create a "solitude basket" filled with items that enhance your alone time experience. This could include a cozy blanket, your favorite book, calming essential oils, or a set of mindfulness cards. Having a dedicated basket creates a visual cue and signifies the start of your solitude ritual.

By establishing a personalized solitude ritual, you prime your mind and body for a deeper dive into self-reflection and rejuvenation. These practices signal the transition into your sacred space of solitude, allowing you to reap the full benefits of your alone time.

Finding Quiet Spaces: Identifying Your Sanctuary

Your environment plays a significant role in shaping your experience. Finding a quiet space that fosters a sense of peace and tranquility is essential for maximizing the benefits of solitude. Look for locations that minimize distractions and allow you to fully immerse yourself in your alone time.

- **Explore Your Home:** Look around your living space with fresh eyes. Is there a quiet corner in your bedroom that could be transformed into a solitude nook? Perhaps your backyard offers a peaceful haven amidst the bustle of daily life. Even a small space can be a sanctuary for solitude with a little creativity.

- **Seek Refuge in Nature:** Nature has a profound ability to promote relaxation and focus. Consider venturing to a nearby park, taking a walk in the woods, or simply sitting on a quiet bench and observing your surroundings. Immersing yourself in nature provides a natural backdrop for introspection and quiet reflection.

- **Utilize Public Libraries:** Public libraries offer a haven of peace, often with designated study areas perfect for solitude. Surround yourself with books and knowledge, and let the quiet atmosphere foster a sense of calm and focus.

- **Coffee Shops (with Caution):** Coffee shops are a double-edged sword. While some offer a vibrant yet peaceful atmosphere conducive to solitude, others are noisy and distracting. Choose a coffee shop known for its tranquility and opt for seating away from the main foot traffic. Be mindful of lingering for too long, as courtesy dictates making space for paying customers.

- **Consider Co-working Spaces:** Co-working spaces often offer dedicated quiet rooms or pods perfect for focused work or solitude. If you work remotely and find it difficult to achieve solitude at home, consider investing in a co-working membership for occasional dedicated alone time sessions.

Actionable Step: Pack a small "solitude kit" to enhance your experience in any location. This could include noise-canceling headphones, an eye mask for deeper relaxation, or a small notebook and pen for capturing thoughts and inspirations. Having a portable kit allows you to create your peaceful haven, even in unexpected environments.

By identifying dedicated spaces for solitude, you create physical and mental boundaries that support your need for quiet reflection. These sanctuaries provide the ideal backdrop for introspection, rejuvenation, and fostering a deeper connection with yourself.

Digital Detoxification: Minimizing Tech Intrusions During Solitude

In today's hyper-connected world, technology is a significant barrier to achieving true solitude. The constant ping of notifications, the temptation to check social media, and the allure of email can disrupt the deep state of relaxation and introspection solitude offers. Here are some strategies for minimizing technology intrusions during your alone time.

- **Embrace Airplane Mode:** The simplest solution is to put your phone on airplane mode during your solitude session. This eliminates notifications and ensures you're not tempted to check emails or social media. If you need your phone for emergencies, consider leaving it in another room to further minimize distractions.

- **Use Do Not Disturb Mode:** Most devices have Do Not Disturb modes that can be customized to silence notifications during specific time frames. Utilize this feature to create a distraction-free zone during your solitude sessions.

- **Invest in a Digital Detox Box:** If you're one of those who find it particularly challenging to resist technology, consider investing in a digital detox box. These lockable containers hold your phone and other devices, creating a physical barrier and preventing you from checking them during your alone time.

- **Communicate with Loved Ones (Optional):** If you're concerned about missing important calls or messages during your solitude session, communicate with loved ones or housemates beforehand. Let them know you'll be unavailable for a specific time frame and that urgent messages can be left through a designated channel, such as a text message to a specific number.

- **Embrace the Power of "No":** Saying no to social media and non-essential communication during your solitude sessions empowers you to prioritize your well-being. Develop a polite response you can use to decline requests that might interfere with your alone time. For example, you could say, "Thank you for the invitation, but I have some dedicated quiet time scheduled for myself this evening. Perhaps we can connect another time?"

Actionable Step: Leave your phone charger in another room. This might seem counterintuitive, but it removes the temptation to "just check one thing" while your phone is charging. Knowing you can't easily access your phone creates a stronger barrier against digital distractions.

By implementing these digital detox strategies, you create a tech-free sanctuary during your solitude sessions. Minimizing distractions allows you to enter a deeper state of relaxation, focus on your inner world, and reap the full benefits of quiet reflection.

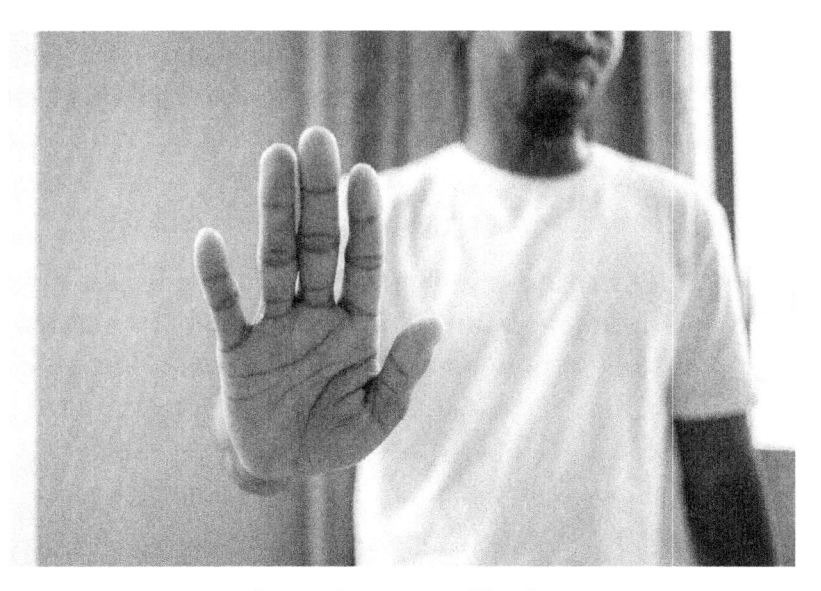

20. Embrace the power of "No". Source: https://www.pexels.com/photo/unrecognizable-black-man-showing-stop-gesture-7114345/

Saying No to Social Obligations: Protecting Your Sacred Time

Social connections are vital for your well-being, but even the most cherished relationships can sometimes encroach upon your need for solitude. Learning to politely decline invitations when you crave alone time is an essential skill for protecting your sacred space.

- **Be Honest and Upfront:** There's no need to make up elaborate excuses. A simple explanation like, "Thank you for the invitation, but I'm prioritizing some quiet time for myself this weekend" is perfectly acceptable. Most people will understand and respect your need for solitude.

- **Offer an Alternative:** If you value the connection but need to prioritize solitude, consider offering an alternative. Suggest meeting for coffee or a short activity another time, demonstrating your desire to connect while protecting your alone time.

- **Set Boundaries with Family:** While family relationships are important, it's equally important to establish boundaries around your need for solitude. Communicate with loved ones about your need for dedicated quiet time, and explore ways to spend quality time together that respect your need for introspection.

- **Practice Saying No:** The more comfortable you become saying no to social obligations that conflict with your solitude needs, the easier it becomes. Role-play with a friend or practice saying no out loud in the mirror to build confidence in asserting your boundaries.

- **Respect the Solitude of Others:** Just as you deserve space for solitude, so do others. Be mindful of imposing on someone else's alone time and respect their need for quiet reflection.

Actionable Step: Schedule your social obligations around your solitude sessions rather than the other way around. Block out dedicated time for alone time in your calendar first, and then schedule social activities in the remaining slots. This approach ensures your needs for solitude are prioritized.

By mastering the art of saying no, you safeguard your sacred space for solitude. Prioritizing your well-being isn't selfish. It empowers you to show up more fully present and engaged in all aspects of your life.

Creating Sacred Spaces for Solitude

The quality of your solitude experience is deeply intertwined with the environment in which it unfolds. Just as a beautiful garden fosters tranquility, a cluttered and chaotic space can hinder your ability to relax and connect with your inner self. This section explores the art of creating sacred spaces for solitude, transforming a simple room into a haven for introspection and rejuvenation.

The Power of Your Environment: Setting the Stage for Inner Peace

Your surroundings have a profound impact on your emotional and mental state. A space designed for solitude, free from distractions and filled with elements that evoke peace and tranquility, can significantly enhance the quality of your alone time.

- **Consider the Purpose:** Before transforming a space, consider how you intend to use it. Do you seek a quiet corner for meditation and reflection? Perhaps you crave a dedicated nook for reading or journaling. Identifying the purpose of your solitude space guides its design and functionality.

- **Trust the Power of Nature:** Nature has the ability to promote relaxation and focus. If possible, situate your solitude space near a window that offers a view of trees, gardens, or even a bustling cityscape (the energy of urban life is invigorating for some). Consider incorporating natural elements like plants, stones, or calming water features into your design. A small tabletop Zen Garden is a particularly meditative addition.

- **Location Matters:** Choose a space that feels separate from the hustle and bustle of your daily life. Ideally, it should be a quiet room with minimal traffic flow. If a dedicated room isn't feasible, consider transforming a secluded corner in your bedroom or living area. Hanging a tapestry or room divider can create a sense of separation within a larger space.

- **Let Light Guide You:** Natural light has a positive impact on mood and well-being. If possible, position your solitude space near a window to benefit from natural daylight. In the evenings, opt for warm, soft lighting that creates a calming ambiance. Dimmer switches allow you to adjust the light level based on your needs and preferences.

- **Embrace the Power of Sound:** Certain sounds can enhance your solitude experience. Consider playing calming music, nature sounds, or white noise to mask distractions and create a peaceful atmosphere. Alternatively, cherish the quiet and allow the silence to deepen your introspection. Experiment with different soundscapes to discover what works best for you.

Actionable Step: Experiment with aromatherapy. Essential oils like lavender, chamomile, and sandalwood have calming properties and can enhance the tranquility of your solitude space. Use a diffuser or place a few drops on a tissue for a subtle yet soothing effect. Consider diffusing citrus essential oils in the morning for an uplifting and energizing atmosphere if you use your solitude space for activities that require focus.

By considering the power of your environment and taking steps to create a space conducive to relaxation, you set the stage for a more profound and enriching solitude experience.

Curating a Calming Atmosphere: Transforming Your Space into a Tranquil Oasis

Once you've identified a dedicated space for solitude, it's time to curate a calming atmosphere that fosters introspection and rejuvenation. Here are some tips for transforming your solitude space into a tranquil oasis.

- **Embrace a Minimalist Approach:** Clutter is visually and mentally overwhelming. Declutter your solitude space, removing unnecessary items and leaving only those that evoke peace and serenity. Clean surfaces and a sense of order will contribute to a more calming atmosphere. Bins and baskets can provide discreet storage for items you might need but don't want to clutter the space.

- **Choose Soothing Colors:** The color palette of your solitude space significantly impacts the ambiance. Opt for neutral tones like pale blues, greens, and grays, which are known to promote feelings of calmness and relaxation. If you prefer color, choose muted tones, or incorporate pops of color through accents like throw pillows or artwork.

- **Comfort is Key:** Ensure your solitude space is comfortable and inviting. Invest in a cozy throw blanket, soft cushions for seating, and perhaps a comfortable chair or yoga mat for meditation or relaxation practices. An adjustable chair allows you to find the perfect position for your chosen activity.

- **Engage Your Senses:** Appeal to your senses beyond sight. Light a scented candle with a calming aroma, diffuse your favorite essential oil, or place a bowl of fresh fruit on a table for a touch of color and fragrance. Consider playing calming music or nature sounds to create a specific ambiance.

- **Personalize with Meaningful Objects:** Surround yourself with objects that hold personal significance and evoke positive emotions. This could be a framed photo of a cherished memory, a collection of inspirational quotes, or a piece of art that resonates with your soul. These personal touches transform your solitude space from a generic room into a sanctuary that reflects your unique personality and fosters a sense of peace and well-being.

Actionable Step: Consider incorporating a "gratitude corner" in your solitude space. This could be a small shelf or table dedicated to displaying items that spark feelings of gratitude. You can have a jar filled with notes expressing things you're grateful for, a collection of postcards from cherished travels, or a small token from a loved one. Surrounding yourself with these reminders of positivity can enhance your mood and deepen your sense of contentment during your alone time.

By curating a calming atmosphere that appeals to your senses and reflects your individuality, you transform your solitude space into a sanctuary for relaxation and introspection. This haven becomes a refuge from the daily grind, a place where you can shed distractions, connect with your inner self, and emerge feeling refreshed and rejuvenated.

Minimizing Distractions: Creating a Haven Free from Interruptions

A core element of a successful solitude space is the absence of distractions. External stimuli can disrupt your focus and hinder your ability to achieve a state of deep relaxation or introspection. Here are some strategies for minimizing distractions in your solitude sanctuary.

- **Silence the Noise:** If possible, choose a quiet location for your solitude space, away from high-traffic areas in your home. Invest in noise-canceling headphones if necessary to block out external sounds. Consider hanging soundproof curtains or tapestries if noise from outside your designated space is a persistent issue.

- **Banish Technology:** The constant ping of notifications and the allure of social media can significantly disrupt your solitude experience. Ideally, leave your phone and other electronic devices outside your solitude space. If you require your phone for emergencies, set it to silent mode and place it face down out of sight.

- **Address Visual Clutter:** In addition to physical clutter, visual clutter can also be distracting. Minimize visual clutter by keeping surfaces clear and avoiding excessive decorations. Opt for calming artwork and photographs over busy patterns or overwhelming displays.

- **Invest in Storage Solutions:** Having designated storage solutions helps keep clutter at bay. Baskets, bins, and shelves provide a place to store items you might need but don't want to clutter your solitude space. A designated charging station outside your solitude space eliminates the temptation to check your phone while seeking solace.

- **Communicate with Loved Ones:** If you share your living space with others, communicate your need for solitude and establish ground rules to minimize interruptions. A simple "Do not disturb" sign on your door or a designated quiet time on your calendar can effectively communicate your need for uninterrupted alone time.

Actionable Step: Consider using a white noise machine to mask external sounds and create a more peaceful ambiance. The constant, low hum of white noise is surprisingly effective in reducing distractions and promoting relaxation.

By minimizing distractions and creating a haven free from interruptions, you empower yourself to fully immerse yourself in your solitude experience. This focused environment allows you to dive deeper into introspection, engage in creative pursuits, or simply unwind and recharge.

Personalizing Your Space: A Reflection of Your Inner World

A truly effective solitude space reflects your unique personality and preferences. By incorporating elements that bring you joy and comfort, you transform it from a generic room into a sanctuary that resonates with your inner self.

- **Embrace Your Favorite Colors:** While calming neutrals are a safe choice, don't be afraid to incorporate pops of color that resonate with you. A favorite accent wall in a soothing yet vibrant hue or colorful throw pillows can add a touch of personality to your space.

- **Infuse Your Space with Inspiration:** Surround yourself with objects that motivate and inspire you. That could be a vision board filled with your aspirations, a quote that resonates with your values, or a bookshelf overflowing with books that spark your curiosity. These visual prompts can serve as a source of inspiration during your alone time.

- **Incorporate Comforting Textures:** Soft throws, plush cushions, and a cozy rug can significantly enhance the comfort level of your solitude space. Surrounding yourself with pleasing textures creates a more inviting atmosphere conducive to relaxation and introspection.

- **Light the Way with Intention:** Consider using lamps with adjustable lighting to create different ambiances. Soft lighting is ideal for relaxation and meditation, while brighter task lighting might be suitable for reading or journaling. Fairy lights or string lights can add a touch of magic and create a more whimsical atmosphere.

- **Embrace the Power of Plants:** Incorporating plants into your living space can reduce stress and promote feelings of well-being. Choose low-maintenance plants that thrive in indirect sunlight, such as snake plants, spider plants, or peace lilies. The natural beauty and calming presence of greenery can significantly enhance your solitude experience.

Actionable Step: Consider incorporating a "comfort object" into your solitude space. This could be a cherished stuffed animal from your childhood, a weighted blanket, or a smooth stone you find calming to hold. These objects can provide a sense of security and comfort, particularly during moments of introspection or reflection.

By personalizing your solitude space with elements that reflect your unique personality and preferences, you create a haven that feels authentically your own. This sense of ownership fosters a deeper connection with your space and enhances the benefits you reap from your alone time.

The Art of Hygge: Creating a Cozy and Comfortable Haven

For a final touch of inspiration, it's time to explore the Danish concept of Hygge (pronounced hoo-gah). Hygge is all about creating a cozy and comfortable atmosphere that promotes feelings of contentment and well-being. Here are some Hygge-inspired elements you can incorporate into your solitude space:

- **Warm Lighting:** Hygge emphasizes warm, inviting lighting. Swap harsh overhead lights for lamps with soft bulbs or string lights to create a more intimate and relaxing ambiance. Candles are another quintessential Hygge element, adding a touch of warmth and flickering light.
- **Cozy Textiles:** Indulge in soft throws, plush cushions, and a comfortable rug to transform your

solitude space into a haven of comfort. Layer textures and patterns for a visually appealing and inviting atmosphere. Consider using natural materials like wool or sheepskin for added warmth and coziness.

- **Warm Beverages:** There's something inherently comforting about a warm drink. Stock your solitude space with your favorite teas, herbal infusions, or hot chocolate. The simple act of preparing and sipping a warm beverage is a calming ritual that enhances your alone time.

- **Indulge in Sensory Pleasures:** Hygge encourages you to embrace sensory pleasures. Light a scented candle with a calming aroma, diffuse your favorite essential oil, or place a bowl of fresh fruit on a table for a touch of color and fragrance. These sensory experiences add richness and depth to your solitude experience.

- **Disconnect to Reconnect:** Hygge emphasizes disconnecting from technology to reconnect with yourself and your loved ones. Leave your phone and other devices outside your solitude space to fully immerse yourself in the present moment and savor the simple pleasures of your alone time.

Actionable Step: Consider creating a "Hygge basket" filled with items that enhance your solitude experience. This could include a cozy throw blanket, your favorite mug, a selection of soothing teas, a book of poetry, and a scented candle. Having a dedicated basket signifies the beginning of your Hygge-inspired solitude ritual.

By incorporating Hygge principles into your solitude space, you cultivate a haven that embodies warmth, comfort, and contentment. This cozy atmosphere allows you to unwind, de-stress, and fully embrace the benefits of your alone time.

Navigating Social Pressures and Expectations

Craving solitude can feel like a rebellion against modern society's constant "go-go-go" mentality. For men, particularly, societal pressures to be social and "always on" can conflict with the need for quiet introspection. This section equips you with strategies for navigating social pressures and expectations, allowing you to embrace solitude confidently without guilt or judgment.

Challenging Societal Norms: Redefining Masculinity to Include Solitude

Traditionally, masculinity has been associated with strength, stoicism, and an aversion to vulnerability. However, this narrow definition leaves little room for the introspective and self-reflective aspects of solitude. Here's how you can challenge the status quo and redefine masculinity to include the need for alone time.

- **Reclaim Your Narrative:** Recognize that the pressure to be constantly social isn't inherently masculine. It's a societal construct. Embrace your need for solitude as a sign of strength and self-awareness, not weakness. Being comfortable in your own company is a powerful form of self-assuredness.

- **Find Role Models:** Seek out and celebrate men who openly embrace solitude and introspection. Authors, artists, athletes, and leaders from all walks of life have utilized solitude as a source of creativity, focus, and renewal. Seeing others you admire prioritizing alone time can empower you to do the same.

- **Educate and Advocate:** Have open conversations with friends and family about the benefits of solitude. Normalize the concept of men needing alone time and challenge the misconception that solitude equates to isolation. By educating those around you, you can chip away at outdated societal norms.

- **Start Small:** Begin by taking small steps towards prioritizing your solitude. Schedule dedicated "me time" in your calendar, even if it's just for 15 minutes initially. As you become more comfortable with solitude, communicate your needs to others and gradually increase the time you dedicate to quiet reflection.

Actionable Step: Challenge the association between masculinity and busyness. Success isn't defined by being constantly on the go. Reframe "busyness" as a badge of inefficiency and prioritize focused work and dedicated time for rejuvenation, including solitude, as key elements of productivity and achievement.

By challenging societal norms and embracing solitude as a masculine strength, you can achieve a more authentic and fulfilling experience of manhood.

Setting Healthy Boundaries with Friends and Family: Communicating Your Need for Alone Time

While social connections are fundamental to well-being, navigating relationships can sometimes feel like a constant tug-of-war between your need for solitude and external demands on your time. Here are some tips for setting healthy boundaries with friends and family and communicating your need for alone time without feeling guilty.

- **Be Honest and Upfront:** There's no need to create elaborate excuses. A simple explanation like, "Thank you for the invitation, but I'm prioritizing some quiet time for myself this weekend" is perfectly acceptable. Most people will understand and respect your need for solitude when communicated clearly.

- **Offer Alternatives:** If you value the connection but need to prioritize solitude, consider offering an alternative. Suggest meeting for coffee or a short activity another time, demonstrating your desire to connect while protecting your alone time.

- **Normalize Solitude:** Normalize solitude in your conversations. Talk openly about the benefits you experience from quiet reflection and introspection. Helping others understand how solitude enhances your well-being fosters empathy and support for your need for alone time.

- **Lead by Example:** Respect the needs of others for solitude as well. When friends or family express a desire for quiet time, avoid pressuring them to socialize. This demonstrates your respect for boundaries and creates a climate of mutual understanding.

- **Communicate Your Expectations:** If you live with roommates or family, establish ground rules regarding your need for solitude. A simple "Do not disturb" sign on your door or designated quiet times on your shared calendar can effectively communicate your need for uninterrupted alone time.

Actionable Step: Practice saying no in a confident yet kind tone. Role-play with a friend or practice declining invitations out loud in the mirror to build the confidence to assert your boundaries effectively.

The Power of "No": Confidently Prioritizing Solitude

Saying no to social invitations can feel daunting, especially when societal norms emphasize constant engagement. However, mastering the art of "no" empowers you to prioritize your solitude needs and create space for the self-reflection and rejuvenation that come with alone time. Here are some actionable steps to confidently decline social invitations when you crave solitude:

- **Focus on "I" Statements:** Frame your refusal around your own needs. Instead of saying, "This doesn't sound like fun," try, "Thank you for the invitation, but I'm prioritizing some quiet time for myself this weekend." This approach avoids negativity and emphasizes your personal need for solitude.

- **Offer Gratitude:** Acknowledge the invitation and express your appreciation. A simple "Thank you for thinking of me" shows your respect for the invitation, even if you're declining.

- **Be Clear and Direct:** Avoid wishy-washy responses or vague excuses. A clear and concise explanation like, "I'm not up for socializing this weekend," is perfectly acceptable. You don't owe anyone detailed explanations for your need for solitude.

- **Suggest Alternatives (Optional):** If you value the connection, offer an alternative way to connect in the future. Suggest meeting for coffee or a quick activity another time, demonstrating your desire to maintain the friendship while prioritizing your solitude needs in the present moment.

- **Practice Makes Perfect:** Role-play declining invitations with a friend or practice saying no out loud in the mirror. Building confidence in your delivery makes it easier to assert your boundaries without feeling awkward or apologetic.

Actionable Step: Consider using technology to your advantage. Many calendars offer features for setting "busy" blocks of time specifically for solitude. Utilizing these features provides a visual cue to others and discourages them from scheduling during your designated alone time.

By mastering the art of saying no, you take control of your schedule and prioritize your well-being. Confidently declining social invitations when you crave solitude empowers you to create the space you need for self-discovery and rejuvenation.

Leading by Example: Normalizing Solitude for Men

Men who openly embrace solitude can have a profound impact on those around them. By normalizing the practice and demonstrating its benefits, you can inspire others to explore the power of alone time for themselves. Here are some actionable steps to lead by example and encourage others to embrace solitude:

- **Be Open About Your Needs:** Talk openly about your need for solitude and the positive impact it has on your life. Sharing your experiences can help others understand that solitude isn't isolation but a valuable tool for self-care and personal growth.

- **Challenge Stereotypes:** Challenge the misconception that masculinity equates to constant busyness. Demonstrate that success is achieved by prioritizing focused work, healthy boundaries, and dedicated time for quiet reflection.

- **Encourage Solitude in Others:** Suggest "solo dates" to friends or family members who might benefit from dedicated alone time. Encourage them to explore activities they enjoy on their own and highlight the potential for self-discovery and rejuvenation.

- **Lead by Action:** Schedule regular periods of solitude into your routine and stick to them. Let others observe your commitment to alone time and witness the positive impact it has on your well-being, energy levels, and overall presence.

- **Celebrate Solitude Success Stories:** When you witness friends or family members embracing solitude with positive results, acknowledge and celebrate their achievements. Sharing these successes reinforces the value of alone time and encourages others to consider exploring its benefits.

Actionable Step: Organize a "Solitude Challenge" with friends or colleagues. Challenge everyone to dedicate a specific amount of time to solitude each week and then come together afterward to share their experiences. This playful approach can spark curiosity about solitude and create a supportive environment for exploring its benefits.

21. Go on "solo dates". Source: https://www.pexels.com/photo/man-writing-in-blank-notebook-in-cafe-7083932/

By leading by example and normalizing solitude, you empower others to challenge societal norms and embrace the power of alone time. Your actions can inspire a shift in perspective, encouraging those around you to prioritize their well-being and discover the transformative potential of quiet reflection and introspection.

Finding Supportive Communities: Surrounding Yourself with Like-Minded Individuals

Surrounding yourself with people who understand and respect your need for solitude is crucial for long-term success. These individuals create a safe space where you can openly express your desire for alone time without judgment. Here are some tips for finding supportive communities that celebrate your introspective nature:

- **Explore Online Groups:** The internet offers a plethora of online communities dedicated to introverts and those who value solitude. Joining these groups allows you to connect with like-minded individuals who share your perspective and experiences. Online forums and social media groups can provide a platform for sharing experiences, exchanging tips on creating a solitary practice, and simply feeling understood. Look for groups specifically geared towards men who value solitude or introverted men's groups to find a community that resonates with your specific needs.

- **Seek Out Local Meetups:** Many cities and towns offer local meetup groups for introverts and solitude enthusiasts. These in-person gatherings allow you to connect with others who share your values and create deeper friendships based on mutual understanding. Meetup.com is a great resource for finding local groups that align with your interests. Look for groups with titles like "Introverts United" or "The Quiet Hour Society" to discover potential communities in your area.

- **Expand Your Social Circles Strategically:** As you navigate your social circles, gravitate towards individuals who appreciate and respect your need for alone time. Seek out friendships with others who value quiet activities, introspection, and meaningful conversations over constant social engagements. These connections will provide a sense of belonging and support within your broader social circle.

- **Don't Discount Existing Relationships:** Some existing friendships might be adaptable to your need for solitude. Talk openly with close friends about your desire for alone time and explore ways to maintain the connection while respecting your need for quiet reflection. Perhaps you can schedule regular phone calls or video chats to stay connected or plan social outings that incorporate periods of quiet activity, such as visiting a museum or enjoying a peaceful hike.

- **Embrace Solo Activities:** Participating in activities you enjoy alone can connect you with a supportive community. Joining a book club, a meditation group, or a nature photography group empowers you to connect with others who share your interests while providing opportunities for quiet reflection and solitude. These shared activities can foster a sense of belonging and camaraderie, even if the interactions are primarily focused on the activity itself.

Actionable Step: Consider starting your own solitude-focused social group. If you struggle to find existing communities that resonate with you, take the initiative to create one yourself. Place an ad online or on local community boards expressing interest in forming a group for men who value solitude. This proactive approach enables you to connect with like-minded individuals and build a supportive community around shared values and experiences.

By actively seeking out supportive communities, you surround yourself with people who understand and appreciate your need for solitude. This support network validates your choices, empowers you to prioritize your well-being, and fosters a sense of belonging that transcends the limitations of societal expectations. Cultivate meaningful connections that enrich your life without compromising your need for quiet introspection and self-discovery.

Throughout this chapter, you've explored the profound benefits of embracing solitude in modern life. From incorporating practical strategies for carving out sacred spaces for quiet reflection to navigating social pressures that might discourage introspection, you've delved into the transformative power of solitude.

Create a sanctuary within to replenish your energy, reconnect with your core values, and cultivate the inner strength to navigate life's complexities with greater clarity and purpose. As you incorporate these practices into your life, you'll discover that solitude is not a luxury. It's a necessity for living a more meaningful and fulfilling life. So, step into the quiet, embrace the gift of solitude, and watch as your inner strength blossoms.

Now, it's time to translate these insights into action. The next chapter provides practical exercises and strategies for cultivating a daily practice of solitude and unlocking the immense potential that lies within.

Chapter 8: The Journey Ahead

The path to self-discovery through solitude is a continuous journey. In the preceding chapters, you've explored the profound benefits of solitude for men, from fostering deeper self-awareness to enhancing creativity and resilience. You've discovered practical strategies for creating sacred spaces for introspection, navigating social pressures, and establishing healthy boundaries to safeguard your alone time.

22. The path to self-discovery through solitude is a continuous journey. Source: https://www.pexels.com/photo/photo-of-man-looking-at-the-mirror-1134184/

Now, as you embark on this ongoing adventure of embracing solitude, it's time to reflect on the personal growth you've experienced, solidify solitude as a lifelong practice, and consider how you might inspire others to discover the power of being alone.

Reflecting on Personal Growth and Transformation

The journey of self-discovery through solitude is a continuous process. Just as a well-worn path deepens with each footstep, your commitment to solitude carves a space for ongoing growth and transformation. In this section, you'll explore strategies for reflecting on the progress you've made, identifying areas for further development, and solidifying your commitment to solitude as a lifelong practice.

Journaling Your Progress: Tracking Your Journey

Journaling is a powerful tool for self-reflection and tracking your growth journey. Dedicating time to journaling during your solitude practice allows you to capture insights, document experiences, and identify patterns that emerge through your engagement with solitude. Here are some actionable steps to incorporate journaling into your solitude practice:

- **Schedule Time for Reflection:** Set aside dedicated time during your solitude sessions for journaling. This focused time allows you to explore your thoughts and emotions without distractions.

- **Start with Prompts:** If you find a blank page daunting, consider using journaling prompts to guide your reflection. Prompts like "What positive changes have I noticed since embracing solitude?" or "How has solitude helped me overcome challenges?" can spark meaningful introspection.

- **Track Your Experiences:** Jot down specific experiences you've had during your solitude practice. Did you experience a breakthrough moment of clarity? Did solitude help you manage stress more effectively? Documenting these experiences allows you to identify the specific benefits you're reaping from alone time.

- **Review and Analyze:** Periodically revisit your journal entries. Analyze recurring themes and identify areas where solitude has had the most significant impact on your life. This reflection process reinforces the positive changes you've experienced and motivates you to continue cultivating your solitude practice.

Actionable Step: Consider creating a dedicated "Solitude Journal" separate from your everyday journaling. This allows you to focus specifically on the insights gained and the progress made through your engagement with alone time.

By incorporating journaling into your solitude practice, you will gain a deeper understanding of your growth journey. Tracking your progress will empower you to celebrate victories, identify areas for improvement, and solidify the positive impact that solitude has on your life.

Identifying Areas for Continued Development: Always Room to Grow

Solitude is a continuous journey of self-discovery. As you progress, use your alone time for ongoing self-reflection and goal-setting. Here are some actionable steps to utilize solitude for continued development:

- **Brainstorming Goals:** Dedicate a solitude session to brainstorming personal and professional goals. The quiet space allows for focused thought and the freedom to explore your aspirations without distractions.

- **Challenge Yourself:** Once you've identified your goals, use solitude to develop strategies for overcoming obstacles and achieving success. The absence of external stimuli allows you to delve deep into challenges and formulate creative solutions.

- **Practice Visualization:** Visualization is a proven method for achieving goals. During your solitude sessions, close your eyes and visualize yourself achieving your desired outcomes. This practice strengthens your commitment and enhances your focus.

- **Track Your Progress:** Monitor your progress towards your goals. Schedule regular solitude sessions to assess your advancement and make adjustments to your strategies as needed. The quiet space paves the way for honest self-evaluation and course correction.

Actionable Step: Consider creating a "Vision Board" for your goals. Include images, quotes, or affirmations that represent your aspirations. Place your vision board in your solitude space as a constant reminder of your goals during your alone time.

By using solitude for ongoing self-reflection and goal setting, you transform your alone time into a springboard for continuous growth and achievement. The quiet space allows you to identify areas for improvement, develop strategies for success, and stay motivated on your personal development journey.

Celebrating Milestones and Achievements: Acknowledging Your Progress

Embracing solitude is a journey filled with triumphs, both big and small. Taking the time to acknowledge your progress is crucial for maintaining motivation and solidifying your commitment to this valuable practice. Here are some actionable steps to celebrate your milestones and achievements:

- **Reflect on Victories:** Schedule dedicated time during your solitude practice to reflect on your victories. Did you overcome a fear of being alone? Did you achieve a personal goal with the help of your solitude practice? Acknowledging these wins reinforces the positive impact of solitude in your life.

- **Reward Yourself:** Celebrating milestones doesn't have to be extravagant. Treat yourself to a small reward after achieving a goal you set during your solitude sessions. This positive reinforcement strengthens the association between solitude and personal growth.

- **Share Your Success (Optional):** Consider sharing your achievements with a supportive friend or family member. Sharing your victories enables them to celebrate with you and reinforces your commitment to your solitude practice.
- **Document Your Journey:** Create a "Solitude Wins" list in your journal. This list is a tangible reminder of your progress and a source of motivation when facing challenges.

Actionable Step: Develop a personal ritual for celebrating milestones. This could be enjoying a cup of your favorite tea in your solitude space, taking a walk in nature, or indulging in a relaxing bath. Associating a positive experience with your solitude practice strengthens its appeal and reinforces its benefits.

By taking the time to celebrate your victories, you acknowledge the progress you've made and solidify your commitment to reaping the rewards of solitude in your life.

The Lifelong Practice of Solitude: A Journey of Self-Discovery

Solitude isn't a temporary fix but a lifelong practice that deepens with each intentional engagement. As you integrate solitude into your routine, view it as a continuous journey of self-discovery and growth. Here are some actionable steps to cultivate solitude as a lifelong practice:

- **Schedule Regular Solitude Sessions:** Block off dedicated time in your calendar for solitude, just like you would schedule any other important appointment. Treating solitude with the same respect as other commitments ensures it remains a consistent presence in your life.

- **Experiment and Adapt:** As your needs and preferences evolve, experiment with different solitude practices and activities. Find what works best for you and adapt your approach over time.

- **Embrace the Journey:** Solitude is a journey, not a destination. There will be times when you crave more alone time and other periods when you desire increased social interaction. Embrace the ebb and flow of your needs and adjust your solitude practice accordingly.

- **Seek Inspiration:** Continue to learn and grow from others' experiences. Read books or articles about solitude, listen to podcasts, or connect with online communities focused on mindful living and introspection. These resources can provide ongoing inspiration and support on your solitude journey.

Actionable Step: Consider creating a "Solitude Toolkit." This could be a physical box or a digital file containing items that enhance your solitude experience. Include inspiring quotes, calming music playlists, essential oils for aromatherapy, or guided meditation recordings. Having a dedicated toolkit readily available empowers you to personalize your solitude practice and maximize its benefits.

By viewing solitude as a lifelong practice, you ensure it remains a cornerstone of your well-being. Scheduling regular sessions, experimenting with different approaches, and seeking ongoing inspiration solidify your commitment to reaping the rewards of alone time throughout your life.

Sharing Your Story: Inspiring Others to Embrace Solitude

The positive impact of solitude isn't meant to be a solitary experience. Sharing your story and insights can inspire others to explore the power of being alone. Here are some actionable steps to share your story and encourage others to embrace solitude:

- **Lead by Example:** The most powerful way to inspire others is to lead by example. Let your commitment to solitude and the positive changes it's brought to your life be evident in your interactions with others.

- **Open Conversations:** Engage in open and honest conversations about your solitude practice. Normalize the concept of needing alone time and dispel any misconceptions others might have about solitude.

- **Share Resources:** Recommend books, articles, or podcasts that have deepened your understanding of solitude. Sharing these resources empowers others to learn more and explore the benefits of alone time for themselves.

- **Organize "Solitude Experiments":** Consider organizing a "Solitude Experiment" with friends or colleagues. Challenge everyone to dedicate a specific amount of time to solitude and then come together to discuss their experiences. This playful approach can spark curiosity and encourage others to consider the value of alone time.

The quiet spaces within hold the potential for profound self-discovery, enhanced creativity, and a deeper connection to your authentic self. The journey of embracing solitude is an ongoing exploration filled with moments of clarity, bursts of inspiration, and the steady hum of personal growth.

Continuing to Embrace Solitude as a Life-long Practice

The need for solitude is a dynamic force that ebbs and flows throughout your life. Just as your priorities and circumstances evolve, so too might your desire for alone time. This section explores how to integrate solitude into your life across different life stages, leverage its power during challenging times, and cultivate a lasting commitment to this enriching practice.

Integrating Solitude into Different Life Stages: A Shifting Landscape

Your need for solitude will likely change as you navigate different life stages. Here are some actionable steps to consider:

- **Young Adulthood:** As you navigate career exploration, independence, and forging your identity, solitude provides a space for self-reflection and decision-making. Schedule dedicated time for introspection to explore your goals, values, and aspirations.

- **Midlife:** During the often-demanding years of midlife, with careers at their peak and families to manage, solitude becomes a crucial sanctuary for rejuvenation. Schedule "digital detoxes" to disconnect from technology and reconnect with yourself. Prioritize quiet mornings or solo walks to clear your head and maintain focus.

- **Later Life:** As life slows down and priorities shift, solitude becomes a source of comfort and creativity. Engage in solo hobbies you may have neglected or dedicate time to journaling and reminiscing.

Actionable Step: Create a "Solitude Vision Board" for each stage in your life. Include images, quotes, or affirmations that represent the type of solitude practice you envision for that period. Review your vision boards periodically to ensure your solitude practice aligns with your evolving needs.

By understanding how your need for solitude might change over time, you can proactively adjust your practice to ensure it continues to provide the support and rejuvenation you need at each stage of life.

Weathering Life's Challenges: A Source of Strength and Resilience

Life inevitably throws curveballs. During difficult times, solitude is a source of strength and solace. Here are some actionable steps to utilize solitude during challenges:

- **Process Difficult Emotions:** Embrace solitude as a safe space to process grief, anger, or frustration. Journal about your feelings, engage in calming activities like meditation or simply allow yourself to cry without judgment.

- **Gain Perspective:** Step away from the chaos and use solitude to gain perspective on challenges. The quiet space allows you to reassess the situation, identify potential solutions, and approach problems with renewed clarity.

- **Boost Resilience:** Solitude is a catalyst for self-care. Engage in activities that nurture your well-being during difficult times, such as spending time in nature, reading inspirational books, or practicing mindfulness exercises.

Actionable Step: Develop a "Solitude Toolkit for Tough Times." This could include a playlist of calming music, uplifting quotes, guided meditations specifically designed for stress management, or a list of comforting activities you can enjoy alone. Having this toolkit readily available empowers you to access the power of solitude quickly when faced with challenges.

By recognizing solitude's potential to provide strength and resilience during difficult times, you can leverage it as a coping mechanism and emerge from challenges feeling renewed and empowered.

23. Process difficult emotions. Source: https://www.pexels.com/photo/sad-man-with-face-in-hands-13801995/

Maintaining a Solitude Routine: Building a Habit of Alone Time

Just like any other beneficial habit, consistency is key to reaping the rewards of solitude. Here are some actionable steps to maintain a regular solitude routine:

- **Schedule It:** Treat solitude with the same respect as important appointments. Block off dedicated time in your calendar for alone time, ensuring it becomes a consistent part of your routine.

- **Start Small:** If you're new to solitude, begin with short periods of alone time and gradually increase the duration as you become more comfortable.

- **Find Your Anchor:** Identify activities you enjoy doing alone, such as reading, taking walks, or listening to music. Associating solitude with these activities makes it more appealing and sustainable.

- **Track Your Progress:** Monitor your progress by keeping a simple journal entry about your solitude sessions. This helps identify patterns and areas where you might need to adjust your routine.

Actionable Step: Develop a pre-solitude ritual. This could be taking a relaxing bath, lighting a scented candle, or simply turning off your phone. This ritual signals the beginning of your dedicated alone time and helps you transition into a more relaxed and reflective state.

By establishing a consistent solitude routine, you ensure it remains a regular part of your life, allowing you to reap the ongoing benefits of quiet reflection and self-care.

Adapting to Change: Evolving Your Practice

Life is in a constant state of flux. As your circumstances change, so too might your need for solitude. Here are some actionable steps to adapt your solitude practice as your life evolves:

- **Be Flexible:** Recognize that your ideal solitude practice might not always be feasible. If life throws you a curveball, be flexible and adjust your approach accordingly. A shorter meditation session might be all you can manage during a busy week, but it's still valuable.

- **Communicate Your Needs:** As your family or living situation changes, openly communicate your need for solitude with those around you. Explain the importance of alone time for your well-being and work together to find solutions that respect everyone's needs.

- **Embrace New Opportunities:** New life stages might present unexpected opportunities for solitude. Traveling solo, taking a weekend retreat, or carving out "me time" during your lunch break can all be enriching experiences of alone time.

- **Revisit Your Vision Boards:** Periodically revisit your "Solitude Vision Boards" for different life stages (created in the "Integrating Solitude into Different Life Stages" section). This empowers you to reassess your needs and adjust your solitude practice to align with your evolving priorities.

Actionable Step: Consider creating a "Solitude Toolbox" specifically for travel. This could be a portable meditation app, a lightweight journal, or a collection of calming nature sounds you can listen to while on the go. Having these tools readily available allows you to incorporate meaningful solitude practices even when your routine is disrupted by travel.

By remaining adaptable and open to modifying your approach, you ensure your solitude practice remains relevant and continues to serve your needs throughout life's ever-changing landscape.

Finding Joy in Being Alone: A Path to Enrichment

Solitude shouldn't be viewed as a deprivation. It is an opportunity for enrichment and personal growth. Here are some actionable steps to cultivate a sense of joy and fulfillment in your alone time:

- **Focus on Activities You Enjoy:** Don't force yourself to engage in solitary activities you dislike. Solitude should be a time for enjoyment and exploration. Prioritize activities that bring you a sense of peace, creativity, or rejuvenation.

- **Practice Gratitude:** Use your solitude practice to cultivate an attitude of gratitude. Reflect on the beauty of the world around you, appreciate the simple joys of life, and express thankfulness for the opportunity for quiet reflection.

- **Embrace the Unexpected:** Sometimes, the most rewarding aspects of solitude arise spontaneously. Be open to new experiences, allow your mind to wander freely, and embrace the unexpected insights that may emerge during your alone time.

- **Connect with Your Inner Self:** Solitude provides a rare opportunity to connect with your authentic self, free from external expectations. Use this time to listen to your intuition, explore your creative potential, and foster a deep sense of self-awareness.

Actionable Step: Develop a "Solitude Bucket List." Brainstorm a list of activities you'd like to try while alone, such as visiting a museum, taking a solo camping trip, or learning a new skill. Having a list of aspirations for your solitude practice adds an element of excitement and anticipation.

By prioritizing activities you enjoy, cultivating gratitude, and embracing the unexpected, you transform solitude from a mere act of being alone into a source of joy, self-discovery, and profound personal enrichment. The most enriching adventures can begin in solitude's quiet embrace.

Inspiring Others to Discover the Power of Being Alone

The benefits of solitude extend far beyond the individual. When you embrace solitude and reap the rewards of self-discovery and well-being, it creates a ripple effect, positively impacting your relationships and the world around you. In this section, you'll explore how you can inspire others to unlock the power of being alone.

The Ripple Effect: Beyond Personal Growth

By prioritizing solitude and nurturing your inner world, you become a more patient, present, and understanding individual. This enhanced well-being translates into positive changes in your interactions with others. Here are some actionable steps to consider:

- **Improved Communication:** Solitude fosters self-awareness and emotional clarity. When you're well-rested and centered, you communicate more effectively with others, fostering stronger and more meaningful connections.

- **Greater Empathy:** Solitude allows you to step outside your perspective and consider the world from a different lens. This fosters empathy and empowers you to connect with others on a deeper level.

- **Enhanced Relationships:** Solitude isn't about isolating yourself from loved ones. It's about showing up for them as your best self. By prioritizing your well-being through alone time, you become a more patient, supportive, and engaged partner, friend, and family member.

- **Positive Influence:** As you embrace solitude and experience its benefits, you become a role model for others. Your positive transformation can inspire those around you to explore the power of alone time for themselves.

24. Your personal growth will echo throughout your life. Source: https://www.pexels.com/photo/water-drop-in-water-in-close-up-photography-3989914/

Actionable Step: Practice active listening during your interactions with others. The quiet reflection cultivated through solitude allows you to be fully present in conversations, offering genuine support and understanding to those around you.

By prioritizing solitude and experiencing its transformative effects, you create a ripple effect of positivity that strengthens your relationships and contributes to a more harmonious world.

Opening Up Conversations: Breaking the Stigma

For men, particularly, embracing solitude can challenge societal norms. Here are some actionable steps to encourage open conversations about the importance of alone time:

- **Normalize the Conversation:** Start by casually mentioning your need for solitude in everyday conversations. Framing it as a form of self-care, not a sign of weakness, normalizes the concept.

- **Lead by Example:** Don't be afraid to express your enjoyment of solitude. Talking openly about the positive impact it has on your life can inspire others to consider its benefits for themselves.

- **Challenge Stereotypes:** Engage in respectful conversations about masculinity that challenge the notion that men should be constantly busy or emotionally unavailable. Promote the idea that strength and well-being are fostered by embracing solitude.

- **Listen and Support:** When others express a desire for alone time, offer support and understanding. Create a space where men feel comfortable discussing their need for solitude without judgment.

Actionable Step: Organize a "Solitude Summit" with a group of male friends or colleagues. This could be a casual gathering where men can openly discuss their experiences with solitude, share tips for incorporating alone time into their lives, and challenge societal stereotypes around masculinity and alone time.

By initiating conversations and challenging outdated norms, you play a crucial role in normalizing solitude and encouraging others to explore its benefits.

Sharing Resources and Tools: Empowering Others

Equipping others with the knowledge and tools to explore solitude is essential in inspiring them to embrace it. Here are some actionable steps to consider:

- **Recommend Books and Articles:** Share books and articles you've found helpful on the topic of solitude. Offer to lend them out or start a book club focused on exploring the benefits of alone time.

- **Podcast Power:** Suggest podcasts or online resources dedicated to self-reflection and introspection. These resources can provide valuable guidance and inspiration for those new to the concept of solitude.

- **Create a "Solitude Starter Kit":** Compile a list of simple activities or exercises that can be done alone, such as guided meditations, journaling prompts, or nature walks. Sharing this list can help others overcome the initial hurdle of figuring out how to spend their alone time productively.

- **Social Media Inspiration:** Consider starting a social media platform dedicated to the positive aspects of solitude for men. Share quotes, tips, and personal experiences to create a supportive online community for those exploring the power of being alone.

Actionable Step: Develop a "Solitude Toolbox App." This app could offer guided meditations specifically designed for men, provide journaling prompts, and suggest solitude activities based on mood or preference. Creating an accessible and user-friendly tool can empower others to easily integrate solitude practices into their lives.

Building a Supportive Community: Strength in Numbers

A supportive community enhances the journey of self-discovery through solitude. Here are some actionable steps to consider:

- **Join Online Groups:** Seek out online communities or forums dedicated to solitude and self-care for men. Connecting with others who understand the challenges and benefits of alone time can provide valuable support and encouragement.

- **Organize Local Meetups:** Consider organizing local meetups for men interested in exploring solitude. These gatherings are a safe space to share experiences, discuss challenges, and celebrate successes on the path of self-discovery through alone time.

- **Mentor Others:** If you've experienced significant personal growth through solitude, consider mentoring others who are just starting their journey. Sharing your insights and offering guidance can empower them to overcome initial hurdles and embrace the benefits of alone time.

- **Advocate for Change:** Advocate for the creation of men's spaces that prioritize well-being and self-care. These spaces could offer workshops on solitude practices, meditation sessions, or simply a quiet environment for men to connect with themselves and each other.

Actionable Step: Partner with local wellness centers or yoga studios to offer workshops or retreats focused on solitude practices for men. This collaboration can provide a safe and supportive environment for men to explore the concept of alone time and its potential benefits.

By fostering a supportive community, you create a space where men feel comfortable exploring solitude, learn from each other's experiences, and celebrate the positive impact of alone time on their lives.

The Future of Masculinity: A Celebration of Wholeness

Imagine a future where embracing solitude is seen as a strength, not a weakness. A future where men are encouraged to prioritize their well-being through self-reflection and introspection. Here are some actionable steps to contribute to this vision:

- **Challenge Stereotypes:** Continue to challenge outdated stereotypes about masculinity. Promote the idea that a well-rounded man prioritizes both connection and solitude, strength, and self-awareness.

- **Support Role Models:** Support and celebrate male role models who openly embrace solitude and self-care. Seeing prominent figures prioritize alone time normalizes the practice and inspires others to follow suit.

- **Advocate for Change:** Advocate for policies and workplace cultures that support healthy work-life balance and encourage men to take time for themselves. Flexible work schedules, dedicated "quiet spaces" in offices, and the normalized use of vacation days can all contribute to a future where solitude is valued.

- **Be the Change:** In the end, your choices today shape the future of masculinity. By embracing solitude and experiencing its transformative effects, you become a living example of a healthy and well-rounded man.

Actionable Step: Consider creating a "Solitude Pledge" for men. This pledge could be a simple statement outlining a commitment to incorporating solitude practices into daily life and challenging societal norms around masculinity and alone time. Encourage others to sign the pledge and join the movement toward a future where solitude is celebrated.

By embracing the lessons gleaned throughout this guide and incorporating these insights into your ongoing journey, you solidify solitude's place as a powerful tool for self-discovery, improved well-being, and a life enriched by meaningful connections and purposeful pursuits. So, take a deep breath, step forward with confidence, and remember that the most enriching adventures often begin in the quiet embrace of solitude.

Conclusion

This book explored the transformative power of solitude for men. It began by dismantling the misconceptions surrounding alone time, revealing it not as a sign of weakness or isolation but as a wellspring of strength, self-discovery, and well-being. Throughout the journey, you explored the psychology of solitude, its impact on various aspects of life, and its ability to ignite creativity and productivity.

You discovered how solitude is a catalyst for cultivating inner strength, resilience, and a deeper sense of self. You uncovered practical strategies for navigating the challenges of incorporating solitude into a modern life filled with constant stimulation and social pressures. Finally, you cast a hopeful gaze toward the future, discovering ways to inspire others to explore the transformative potential of being alone.

Key Takeaways

- **Solitude is a Sanctuary, Not a Prison:** Distinguish between solitude, a time for focused introspection and self-renewal, and loneliness, the emptiness that can accompany social isolation. Embrace solitude as a sanctuary where you shed societal expectations and reconnect with your authentic self.

- **Benefits Beyond the Self:** The benefits of solitude extend far beyond the individual. By prioritizing your well-being through alone time, you cultivate emotional regulation, improved self-awareness, and enhanced creativity. These qualities enrich your own life and also the lives of those around you.

- **Stronger Relationships, Deeper Connections:** Solitude isn't about retreating from loved ones. It's about showing up for them as your best self. By prioritizing your well-being through alone time, you become a more present, patient, supportive partner, friend, and family member, fostering stronger and more meaningful connections.

- **Fueling the Creative Spark:** Solitude provides a fertile ground for fostering new ideas, sparking inspiration, and allowing creativity to flourish. Free from distractions and external pressures, you can delve into your imagination, explore new perspectives, and bring innovative solutions to the surface.

- **Building Inner Strength, Not Walls:** Embrace solitude as a tool for cultivating resilience, processing difficult emotions, and developing a deeper sense of self-worth. In the quiet space of solitude, you confront challenges head-on, gain clarity on your values, and emerge stronger and more confident.

- **A Lifelong Practice, Not a Temporary Fix:** Integrating solitude into your life is an ongoing journey, not a one-time destination. As your circumstances and priorities evolve, adapt your solitude practice to ensure it continues to serve your needs throughout different life stages.

- **Inspire Others, Challenge the Norm:** Share your positive experiences with solitude and challenge societal norms around masculinity and alone time. Be a role model for others, demonstrating that embracing solitude is a sign of strength, not weakness, and a fundamental pillar of healthy masculinity.

This journey of self-discovery through solitude is a continuous, lifelong exploration that unfolds with each dedicated moment of alone time. By incorporating the practices and strategies outlined in this book, you'll unlock the transformative power of being alone and cultivate a life enriched by meaningful connections, personal growth, and a profound sense of well-being.

Have you embraced solitude in your life? How has it impacted you? Leave a review and share your story to inspire others on their path of self-discovery through the power of being alone. Your voice will contribute to a future where embracing solitude is celebrated as a cornerstone of a fulfilling and enriching life for men.

References

Heideman, J. (2021, June 28). How to Practice Solitude. The Daily Grace Co. https://thedailygraceco.com/blogs/the-daily-grace-blog/how-to-practice-solitude

Howard, D. (n.d.). Ten Reasons We Should Practice Solitude | Full Strength Network. Fullstrength.org. https://fullstrength.org/ten-reasons-we-should-practice-solitude/

Marie, V. (2020, July 7). Practicing silence & solitude • Val Marie Paper. Val Marie Paper. https://www.valmariepaper.com/how-to-practice-silence-solitude/

PhD, A. W. (2020, June 15). Practicing Solitude. Www.productiveflourishing.com. https://www.productiveflourishing.com/p/practicing-solitude

Rodriguez, D. G. (2016, November 21). Simple Ways to Practice Solitude Daily. Medium. https://medium.com/@dekerag/simple-ways-to-practice-solitude-daily-56ee1415632

The Spiritual Practice of Solitude. (2021, October 15). Preston Gillham - Author. https://www.prestongillham.com/blog/the-spiritual-practice-of-solitude

Verve. (2019, June 5). How to Practice Spiritual Solitude - Spiritual Disciplines. NIV Bible. https://www.thenivbible.com/blog/how-to-practice-solitude/

Printed in Great Britain
by Amazon